# WHAT WE HAD

A MEMOIR BY

## James Chace

SUMMIT BOOKS

NEW YORK • LONDON • TORONTO
SYDNEY • TOKYO • SINGAPORE

SUMMIT BOOKS
Simon & Schuster Building
Rockefeller Center
1230 Avenue of the Americas
New York, New York 10020

Copyright © 1990 by Chacecorp, Inc.
All rights reserved
including the right of reproduction
in whole or in part in any form.
SUMMIT BOOKS and colophon are
trademarks of Simon & Schuster Inc.
Designed by Edith Fowler
Manufactured in the United States of America

10  9  8  7  6  5  4  3  2  1

Library of Congress Cataloging in Publication Data

Chace, James.
    What we had : a memoir/by James Chace.
    p.   cm.
    1.  Chace, James—Childhood and
youth.   2.  Journalists—United States—
Biography.   3.  Fall River (Mass.)—Social life
and customs.
    I.  Title.
PN4874.C595A3   1990
070'.92—dc20                              89–78431
[B]                                          CIP

ISBN 0-671-69478-2

    Poem on p. 13 excerpted from "Turn (2): After Years" from The Messenger by
Jean Valentine. Copyright © 1979 by Jean Valentine. Reprinted by permission of
Farrar, Straus and Giroux, Inc.
    Poem on p. 82 excerpted from "East Coker" in Four Quartets, copyright 1943
by T. S. Eliot and renewed 1971 by Esme Valerie Eliot, reprinted by permission
of Harcourt Brace Jovanovich, Inc.
    Poems on p. 83 and p. 103 reprinted with permission of Macmillan Publishing
Company from The Poems of W. B. Yeats: A New Edition, edited by Richard J.
Finneran. Copyright 1940 by Georgie Yeats, renewed 1968 by Bertha Georgie
Yeats, Michael Butler Yeats, and Anne Yeats.
    Lyrics appearing on p. 88 from "I Get a Kick out of You" by Cole Porter. © 1934
WARNER BROS. INC. (Renewed) All Rights Reserved. Used By Permission.

*This book is for*
*Sarah, Rebecca and Zoe Chace,*
*and for Michael Denvir.*
*And for Lois and Gardner.*

# Acknowledgments

---

I am grateful beyond measure to Bertha Harris and to Lis Harris for their careful reading of the manuscript at every stage of its writing.

Others whose criticisms, suggestions and encouragement have helped me in the composition of this book are Renata Adler, Harry Atkins, John Bowers, Caleb Carr, Rebecca Chace, Sarah Chace, Camilla Clay, Harvey Ginsberg, Phyllis La Farge, Nora Sayre, J. G. Sherman, Joseph Spieler and Mark Uhlig.

My editors, James Silberman and Anne Freedgood, have provided invaluable editorial judgment and profound support.

Lois Chace McManus has spoken to me at length about family history and events that took place so many years ago. She has helped connect the threads of this narrative.

# Contents

*"I think of our lives*
*different        the same*

*the years, half blown,*
What we had, we have."

Turn (2):  After Years,
JEAN VALENTINE

# Burying
# Holly and Mildred

My mother lies in an unmarked grave. I had never meant to keep her there for long— but it was what I could afford at the time. My father lay nearby, his grave absurdly identified by a flat marker that the veterans had placed there, though my father served in the army only a few months—Pvt. Hollister R. Chace, Stu. Army Tng. Corps, World War I. I let that happen for the same reason—because I didn't think I could afford a decent stone. The graves themselves were in the Hawkins plot, Aunt Sue's husband's family. Which seemed somehow appropriate given the more recent history of the Chaces. Sue, after all, had married money, cotton money, as it turned out, from Dick Hawkins' cotton brokerage. And the Chaces, not surprisingly, had grown dependent on her income for odd handouts for recurring emergencies, so dependent, it seems, that Uncle Dick grew to dread visits of his wife's family—my father, my aunts and uncles, their children, my brother and me, the scavengers of chocolate patties and after-dinner mints.

When my father died, my cousin suggested that I could save some money if I went up to the Oak Grove Cemetery, the great burying ground of Protestant Fall River, and saw if anything was left in the Hawkins plot. Daddy's insurance came to almost nothing, I was newly married and making do with two small children, and my brother was working in South America and deliberately distant from us. As I might have expected, there were at least four grave-sites available. The plot itself was in an elegant spot, near the main gate, shadowed by broad oak trees. In any case, we had to settle the business quickly after my father died of a heart attack.

As the years passed, I always intended to do something about the unmarked grave and the unseemly military marker. I felt humiliated having them there, even if no one knew or cared, a neglectful son after all. Somehow I had to make the effort to put things right, perhaps because I didn't want to disappear as they had. I simply had to get them out of the Hawkins plot altogether and over to Swansea, a town nearby where all the other Chaces were buried, and give them their own headstone. It was characteristic of my mother's connection to the family that her name should be effaced, just what the Chaces might have expected, and that she should lie in the Hawkins plot, just what she might have expected when we buried her husband there two years earlier.

In the beginning—before she ever met the Chaces, before the First World War—Mildred Clarke came to Fall River, Massachusetts, from Wappingers Falls, New York, a fifteen-year-old girl with long blond hair and a ribbon fixed in its tresses. I wish I knew my mother's first impressions as she saw the city rise on the hill above the Taunton River. Smoke belching from the hundred and forty cotton mills would have made the sky grimy. Nonetheless, the vastness of Mount Hope Bay where the waters were so deep ocean-going steamships could ply the rivers from Newport to Fall River might have pleased her. But my grandmother, Hattie Clarke, standing at the rail of the New York boat, saw the darkness of the mills and must have hated what she saw. She must have heard tales of the cruelty of factory life in New England in 1914, and even though her husband was a skilled engraver, the conditions of life in Fall River would have sickened her. She had never wanted to leave the comfortable streets of

Wappingers Falls; she loved the drama of the
Hudson River, all forested over along the river-
banks.

My grandmother never told me directly
that she dreaded coming to the city, but night
after night I used to go to sleep beside her, and
all her stories were of the same distant landscape where headless horsemen rode through
the lush valleys of Tarrytown. There was a high
fourposter in her room, not wide enough to
qualify as a double bed but broad enough for
Grandmother and me, so that I drifted off to
sleep with her voice, soft and very steady, in
my ear. In the corner were my grandfather's
engraving tools in the metal box that sat beside
my grandmother's foot-driven Singer sewing
machine that she had used when she worked as
a seamstress in those dark years just before Jim
Clarke came into her life. "Tell me about the
Hudson Valley again," I asked. About her
brothers and sisters, about the poor Dutch of
the Hudson Valley whose children had to leave
school in the golden age of robber barons after
the Civil War.

They say Jim Clarke laughed a lot. And
that was good for my grandmother. Having em-
igrated to Canada from Manchester, England,
in 1884, my grandfather came down the Hudson
a journeyman engraver and married Hattie
Maccabe. He had one good eye that could work

the tools; the other eye was glass. Jim had been
playing in the factory in Manchester, taunting,
taunted, and looked up the chute at his tormen-
tor. A steel-tipped shuttle dropped, sped
through the narrow tunnel, and put out his eye.
Nonetheless, he came to earn a good living, and
where was there a better place to prosper than
Fall River on the eve of the First World War? So
my grandmother took the boat from Poughkeepsie to New York with Mildred's hand
tightly clasped in hers and then the Fall River
Line to Newport and Mount Hope Bay and the
booming Spindle City.

She lived thirty-five years without making
a friend in this city she always distrusted, taking the Fall River boat back once a month to
Poughkeepsie with her only daughter to visit
her beloved brothers and sisters. Her husband
worked at the seemingly impregnable American
Print Works. Their house looked out over the
Taunton River from a gentle prospect on Walnut Street. Somewhere between prosperity and
simply making a decent living.

Mildred was willowy and quick, and her
hair trailed golden as she ran up the hill to
school. It was when she was sixteen that she
met Holly Chace, first at a dance at the amusement park. As she put it in her diary on June
22nd, 1915: "I went to a dance and met an aw-
fully nice fellow called Hollister Chace." By

September she was writing: "I think he loves me." He wrote a poem about her—"the girl he met in Lincoln Park / Whose name was Mildred Clarke / And when we danced / She put me in a trance / I met her after a day or so / And again she set me all aglow / And I love her because she is a Jersey cow."

"Your mother," I was told, "was always smart. Like her mother." Her mother bought the Encyclopedia Britannica and read it through to educate herself after she left school for a sweatshop in Poughkeepsie. Mildred was probably smarter than her boyfriend and certainly better looking. Holly had the baggy Chace eyes and large nose, but he grew a moustache sometime after the war and his hair went gray and his clothes fit easily and he looked as handsome as the playboy he was surely fit to be.

My mother's problem for the Chaces was her own modest background, and that she came from nowhere. There were richer families in Fall River, but the Chaces had been around. They had been treasurers of mills and sea captains, and Holly's father was Frank Minthorn Chace, the President of the Massachusetts State Senate. Moreover, he had married well when he found Amanda Livingstone Dubois from New York City. The Duboises had money, and plenty of it, owned large tracts of what became Central

Park, even operating a racetrack in upper Manhattan. My grandparents produced twelve children in all, though six of them died in one week of black diphtheria in 1889.

By the time my mother got to know the family, there were only six left—three brothers, Fred, who had already left for a position with the New Haven Railroad, Gardner and Holly, and their sisters, Sue, Ellen and Mabelle. The Senator had spent or was spending most of the Chace money on his singularly successful political campaigns. He'd been in the Senate for years, and before that County Commissioner, and was planning to run for Congress after the war. None of the sons had yet married, but apparently the daughters had behaved commendably—Sue had wed a Hawkins, and Ellen and Mabelle seemed to have done as well. For Holly and his brother Gardner it was a different matter. They were younger and the war was on. Gardner went to France and fought at Château Thierry. A letter to his father was published in the paper: "If the Boches want fight and still more fight, they will get it good and plenty. With Turkey and Austria out of the way, the allied armies will simply surround them and then, no more Germany. Tell Holly to get in the game."

But my father was the youngest, the mischief maker, who had thrown horse manure from a treetop down on his sister Mabelle and her new husband, as they drove to Providence in an open cabriolet. My father did not choose to enlist but stayed behind to court my mother. The Senator didn't approve of this. The sisters, too, seemed imperious to my mother. Ellen was forever telling her how to dress, how to wear her hair. True, my mother had no real money, but her beauty was such that she never had to wear makeup; her cheeks were tinged with red and her lashes were shadowy, and her voice was delicate, as though she would break with rough handling.

The Senator thought his son might grow stronger if he went into the army, got into the game, and that he might reconsider his courtship of Mildred Clarke for someone with more money. It was 1918 by then, and my father was only 19, and it was fitting that he should join up to satisfy his father and his older brother. He finally went to Holy Cross College, to officers' training school, to "fight the battle of College Hill," as he put it. When the war ended, he had been there less than three months, not time enough to earn his commission. Mildred and he would be married within the year.

September 16th, 1919. From my mother's diary—"Married at four at the church. Everything beautiful. Left on the boat for New York."

The next day—"The Hippodrome in the afternoon. Slept at the Astor. Left for Wappingers Falls in the morning." By New Year's Eve, she could write—"The end of the year. It has been a wonderful year to me. Holly is doing fine in business and I am very happy."

My brother Hollister was born in 1921, and his mother didn't see him for three weeks. She almost died of hemorrhaging and wouldn't have had the strength to nurture him. But my grandmother was there. She took care of things, for the young couple had set up house with Mildred's parents. The arrangement was surely never meant to be permanent. My father was working in one of the mills my grandfather had an interest in and was also involved in liquidating mills during the recession in the New England textile industry that had come just after the war. There was money to be made in the South, he could see that, what with the new mill towns in the Carolinas and Georgia where there were no unions and the equipment was mint new.

But there was a fatal ease in my father's approach to life, a kind of carelessness that let things fall. Staying with Hattie and Jim Clarke vastly pleased him. Though he didn't bring in much of a regular salary, a sudden sale of heddle frames or spindles yielded a windfall of

happiness: a new coat for his wife, trains for
little Hollister, a round of drinks at the Tiverton
Yacht Club.

My mother was bewildered. She was
twenty-two and Hollister's birth, her doctors
told her, left her unable to conceive again.
There was no need to practice birth control. My
father liked company—picnics and dinner parties, card games and polo. He was really best at
horses, either in the saddle or at the track, so
good in fact that he played for the Newport polo
team. My mother went along with him. Perhaps
she was too much in love with him to bother
much with Hollister, and this was made easier
by her mother's attention to all the details of
housekeeping—the homemade doughnuts, the
shepherd's pie, Welsh rarebit on a Sunday evening. When money was short, her mother
showed her how to make a yummy supper out
of a can of Campbell's tomato soup: no water
added and American cheese cooked until the
cheese blended in and then poured over
Uneeda biscuits. She christened it Blushing
Bunny, and it became a family staple.

My father and mother had good times in
the twenties—even as the textile industry col-
lapsed. There were friends galore and money to
spare, at least so long as Jim Clarke's job held
at the American Print Works. As they seemed
to flourish, the Chace sisters got divorced. Aunt

Ellen had been too demanding of clothes and jewelry; when the Senator died in 1921, Ellen realized that without money from Papa her husband couldn't give her what she wanted. Aunt Mabelle and her husband simply went into debt. I was told they avoided the creditors by keeping the shades drawn in their house all week long and raising them on Sundays when it was forbidden to serve a summons.

The Senator's death left everyone at sea. He willed his wife seven diamond rings and a tower of debt—the legacy of his political campaigns, his trips to Florida, his houses in Tiverton, Rhode Island, and Nantucket. The diamond rings didn't stay in the family long. Soon after selling them, my grandmother ended up in an apartment house in Fall River—and later with Ellen—until she died in 1936. With the Senator's death, Ellen and Mabelle especially seemed to have lost their bearings, and Gardner and Holly drifted ever more willfully. Gardner's automobile dealership foundered. Unlike Holly he had no father-in-law to underwrite those soft afternoons in Tiverton or Newport. There was, nonetheless, an odd glamor to the chaos: Ellen dressed ever more extravagantly and grew ever more beautiful, and Mabelle's marriage broke up in a tangle of smashed sports cars and flapper parties that always seemed to end at dawn. By the end of the decade both sisters were remarried, Mabelle to an insurance broker who led her into a reclusive life in a seaside town outside New Bedford, and Ellen to Theodore Mark, known as Shockie, a corruption of Chockey from a childhood mispronunciation of the word chocolate. A great athlete, he had barely hung up his basketball shoes when he was already involved in at least two business deals—obtaining a franchise for a rollerhockey team and buying into the Narragansett race track. Their daughter was born very soon after their marriage, which left Ellen unaccustomedly alone while Shockie spent many too many nights at the Fall River Casino at some sporting event.

Sue alone enjoyed prosperity. With Dick Hawkins, she lived in a large house across the state line in Tiverton that had fields running down to the river and a stable of horses, grape arbors, wild raspberry patches, lilacs and chrysanthemums, a burning bush, patches of violets, and day lilies sprawling beyond the verandah down to the barn. Since Sue was well into her forties before marrying Dick, there were no children, but the horses and cats filled the landscape. Sue was mostly alone in her lovely house. Increasingly, Dick sought golf trophies from ever more distant country clubs. The cotton brokerage no longer made money as it once did in those halcyon years before the collapse of the textile industry after the war.

Accustomed to handouts and with nothing to spare, my parents were hardly touched by the stock market crash. Then in 1931, I was born. A kind of miracle after my mother had been told she could have no more children, that she would likely not survive another birth. Yet, as she told me often enough, "I was drinking a martini at the Stone Bridge Inn less than a week after you were born." I imagine that my brother grew to hate my unexpected birthday, "ten years to the day after his own," as my grandmother put it. Hollister was no longer "our heart's dearest." Except perhaps to his grandfather, Jim Clarke, who took him everywhere. To the bar at Fa-Neek's where Hollister was put on a high stool and given a short beer. To the shellfish bar at Westport Point. Hand in hand with Jim Clarke to the inner courtyard of the print works so that he could gaze straight up into the face of its enormous clock.

But then in 1934 the American Print Works closed. Despite the erosion of the textile industry that had begun in 1919 (the millowners had set nothing aside for capital improvements, as though the belt-driven overhead looms would last another fifty years), this city of brick and gray granite gave the illusion of being anchored to Fall River's emblem of perpetual security, the great clock tower of the American Print Works. Even before the fall of the print works, the city went into bankruptcy. Fall River's finances were to be run by the state, and my grandfather found himself out of a job.

He was in his sixties by then but, after all, he was an engraver. His tools cut a die as sharp as the needle on my grandmother's sewing machine. Of course there was work, even in 1934, and if a man could emigrate from Manchester, England, to Poughkeepsie, New York, and to Fall River, Massachusetts, he could emigrate again. It didn't take my grandfather long to find work. One trip south was enough. He found just the job in Columbia, South Carolina. As soon as he rented a house for us all, we would follow. But then, what of my father? I think he was bewildered at events. His own business was actually being nourished by the failing mills as he sold more and more machinery to Athens, Georgia. But equally significant, my parents had become accustomed to living in Jim Clarke's benevolent light and shadow. The terrible thing happened while my mother was giving a bridge party. I was three years old, unaccountably asleep, for I was a cranky, nervous child. It was a telegram, and it said that he had died in a car crash, thrown from a rumble seat in South Carolina.

My mother and father tried to go on as they
had before, but my brother Hollister had lost
his world. In the blindness of adolescence, he
perceived a connection between the "miracle"
of my birth and his loss of the single person
who had loved him without reserve. While I
continued in my grandmother's embrace, which
would never end, Hollister began to strike out
at me.

Soon after, what was left of our own family
started to spend the summers in a cottage that
lay at the foot of Aunt Sue's land. It was stuck
up on piles on the river, its beach a shoal of
scallop shells and barnacled rocks. From the
porch you could look across to the Hummocks
and see the sunset, the hour when my father
would row me in the skiff to the middle of the
Sakonnet River and dump the perishable gar-
bage for the seagulls to spirit away. But what
was my brother doing in those years just before
the 1938 hurricane that I have so little memory
of him? A blackness bars his image. Yet he was
also present, sleeping beside me in the maple
twin bed. Did he touch me in the night? Did he
beat up on me in the darkness? He could never
remember me either, he confessed years later.
Alone on the porch, my mother drank
throughout still afternoons while I played below
her at the river's edge. I could see water rats at

the pilings, black, gleaming, and in the river
islands that appeared both alluring and threatening, Dr. Doolittle islands stocked with exotic
beasts. On Sundays, we would wander up the
hill to Aunt Sue's house.

I especially liked playing in the grape arbor
and sucking the fruit off the black skins, and
sometimes as I hid in the leafy shadows I would
hear my father or my Uncle Gardner asking
Aunt Sue for money. I was told later she used
to hock her diamond rings for them when Uncle
Dick was away and could not notice.

The end of the 1930s summers came just
after we had moved back to the city, so I could
get ready for school before Labor Day. It was
1938, the year that the hurricane swept up from
the Florida keys and hit Narragansett Bay and
the Sakonnet River at the very moment of high
tide. The winds didn't seem so bad at first. But
then my father came to get me as I walked home
along June Street. By late afternoon trees were
falling. We huddled in the living room of
friends. Everyone was drinking and fearful,
and I remember the chimney cracking and the
bricks tumbling off the roof. The wind surrounded us; it did not howl or whistle but came
at us like an immense battering ram.

The next day the streets were littered with
trees, great sprawling elms that made a kind of
copse that you could play in. It was days before

we could drive to Tiverton to see about the summer cottage. We were already alarmed because
the hurricane had been accompanied by a tidal
wave, and the fierceness of the winds, com-
bined with the rising moon tide, had ripped
enormous summer houses at Westport Harbor
from their very foundations. The wave rolled
down the Sakonnet River and swept the shore
clean. There was nothing left of our cottage but
a wrought-iron magazine rack Hollister had
made in junior high school. We drove up the
hill to Aunt Sue's place, looked out over the
broken arbor and the barren gardens, and
the grown-ups started drinking that afternoon,
and drank until night fell, when they found my
mother wandering in the barn among the horses
she had always been frightened of.

Throughout the second war we went to
Aunt Sue's again and again. To eat and to argue
and, of course, to borrow money. To avoid the
scene Uncle Dick stopped having Sunday dinners and then died of a stroke at the seventh
hole. He had just chipped the ball with a nine-
iron onto the green and it looked as if another
birdie was in the offing. Aunt Sue might have
flourished with Dick's death. Instead, she remained in Tiverton in the big house and tried
to live as she had always lived, afraid to disturb
the regular order of things while her brothers

and sisters flocked about her with increasing demands on her money. She even financed my father's campaign for the city council.

The war seemed to bring all the grown-ups low. Maybe it was having Hollister and young Gardner away in the army. With her son gone, Uncle Gardner's wife, who had never come with us to Dick and Sue's, languished in her bed, drinking black coffee and reading stories by Edgar Allan Poe. Uncle Gardner himself disappeared for long stretches, and it was said he was having an affair with another woman. With Hollister gone, my own life flickered more brightly, but my mother shrank into herself. It was Pearl Harbor that brought an end to the carelessness of my parents' lives, the war and the sight of their son boarding a train on a foggy cold February morning, a son whom they had let go without quite knowing what they had been holding. Hollister spent almost four years in combat in the South Pacific. He never got one day's leave to visit us before he was shipped out to Seattle and then Australia.

My mother drank most of the day now. A glass not much bigger than a jigger held her lemon-flavored gin. She would place it on a pantry shelf, and its amber glow came up higher in the late afternoon sunlight. My father was away much of the time, perhaps with other women or working at extra jobs. Sometimes he would come in late at night after my mother had taken me to bed with her, and he would scoop me up in his arms and carry me, half-asleep, into the adjoining room.

Then, for a moment after the war, there was a surge of hope, and it came, as it had for so long now, from the Hawkinses. Aunt Sue had had a small stroke, and the house had to be sold and all the land, and we were all to share in the profits. Imagine a Sunday afternoon in 1946. My father and mother, Uncle Shockie and Aunt Ellen, Uncle Gardner, and Aunt Sue are all on the back porch. Neither the cousins nor Hollister, back from the war and still living with us, bother to show up for the Sunday dinners any more. The striped awning has been set out to keep the sun away. You can look down over the day lilies, past the grape arbor to the empty barn and across to the Sakonnet River and the Hummocks. A Candy Boat race is in progress: twelve-foot marconi-rigged catboats are rounding the buoy just on the port side of the railroad bridge. Ellen: "Well, there it is, everything we could have expected."

Holly: "Thirty thousand dollars."

Gardner: "In cash."

Shockie: "What's wrong with you people? Don't you trust the banks?"

The house itself is almost empty. Tomorrow Sue moves to the city. She will live near

Ellen. Thirty thousand dollars in cash. Gardner decides to pour champagne. Someone says, "I'll put the money away for safekeeping."

It is a hot day, a day nonetheless for roast turkey and summer squash and stuffing and broccoli and cranberry sauce. Sue is thinking that now she has come to the end of hocking diamond rings for them. This will give them what they want. A new start. A clean slate.

My mother sips a Tom Collins. Tries to recall something. The river below is placid, and the Hummocks are hardly more than sand dunes. Not like the Hudson, not so dramatic. She is tired of being alone at night while my father works for a liquor store or tends bar or goes out with someone else.

"Where's the money?"

"What happened to the money?"

The thirty thousand dollars, the neat packages of thousand-dollar bills with rubber bands to keep them together, are gone as though a magician had passed his hand over them and they had disappeared into a box with a false bottom. The tabletop where the money stood is bare now.

Shockie leaps up the stairs three at a time. My father ransacks the cartons stacked up in the living room. Gardner crawls on his hands and knees through the dining room. Sue and Ellen walk about touching window sills. My mother tries to help but subsides into a rocking chair. Then she smells something burning. Like leaves in the fall. The odor of these burning leaves or petals becomes mixed up with the roast turkey and the stuffing, and she remembers no one bothered to make the gravy, or perhaps there was no flour, but there's something wrong.

So my mother pushes herself up from the rocker and takes another sip of her Tom Collins and walks into the kitchen. She sees the smoke rising from the oven, wispy smoke drifting up, and the smell of roasting turkey is fainter now because of that burning smell. She just lurches forward and pulls open that oven door and there they are, on the upper rack, just above the basting turkey, those thirty thousand dollars, flaming at the edges where someone had put them to hide them away because they wanted the actual cash, not just a check, and my mother puts her delicate white hands into the oven and sweeps that money, some five thousand dollars gone, onto the kitchen floor and pours Tom Collins mix all over it.

When my father died in 1965, people asked me if I dared let my mother live alone. It was certainly an unpromising situation. With alcohol mother was out of key with her time and didn't make much sense. Her words wandered,

and our conversation followed no logic. Even
the weather. "What's it going to be like tomorrow, Jimmy?" "Clear and cold and plenty of
sunshine." "I don't understand how you can live
in New York." That was another problem. How
could I bring her to New York, to an apartment
on West 110th Street, to the long dark hallway
that led to the tiny room reserved, before my
time, for the live-in maid, to the noise of two
little girls, eight and six, and my wife trying to
cope with them and no money? How could I
myself cope with mother's nighttime drinking
and no friends and trying not to get mad at her?

"Things have a way of sorting themselves
out." That's what my mother once told me after
Aunt Ellen had her first stroke and her daughter Lois moved her down south to be with her
and the children a little too soon, and Ellen just
kept on living and driving everyone a little bit
crazy. "Things have a way of sorting themselves
out," I said after my father died. I left my
mother in Fall River with these words. She lived
in a tiny apartment not far from my cousin
Gardner. Every day he sent one of his boys
down to see what Mildred needed: cigarettes,
shrimps, cans of pea soup, Roma wine. My
brother was living in Peru running a textile mill
for an American company and hadn't been able
to come home for my father's funeral. It was

just as well, for we might have fought over the
style of the coffin or the hours of the wake.

It didn't take too long for things to get
sorted out. One of Gardner's boys found her
passed out on the floor, her head cut open.
There wasn't much to do but move her to the
hospital, and it turned out her hip had broken
in her fall. I went to see her right away, but I
couldn't talk to her. She was tied down in a bed
shaking, crying and shaking, small and shriv-
eled. There was nothing to do but let it pass. It
didn't look as if she would survive, such a rag-
ged thing as she was, but she did, and through
her delirium she seemed to shake off the eternal
childhood that had been imposed on her.

There wasn't any money, so I put her on
the Massachusetts Old Age, designed for the
helpless and the indigent. We moved her into a
nursing home till her hip mended and she could
go into an apartment of her own. The hip did
mend, but one day she woke up and found
blood between her legs, and it was cancer. She
never complained much. The nurses liked her
for that. Later she had to go to Boston for radia-
tion. I went to see her at that other hospital and
she said it was awful, just awful.

But something happened in the eighteen
months before she died. I grew to love her
again, or perhaps for the first time, because for

so many years she had been a ghost, turned into herself. Even as a little boy I looked to my grandmother Clarke for the hot doughnuts after school and the careful reading of a school paper. Later, as my father failed and my mother could hardly string sentences together, I sometimes lashed out at her, and she looked at me with bewildered eyes. But the eyes were clear now. Deprived of alcohol, she became lucid, funny, brushing aside all the trivial details of shabby clothes and overcooked meals. We drove to restaurants that overlooked the sea and played songs on the juke box that my father used to like. Her grandchildren played about her in the deep grass in front of the barn we rented that summer. She played endless card games of Spit with them, and we made plans for a visit to New York when she could go with them to the Central Park Zoo and watch the seals play.

Under her sickness her face showed deep lines for the first time, and the blush-red cheeks turned mottled red, and the auburn hair grayed at the edges. Yet she emerged in those final days with an affecting love, as though she had walked through a gauzy mosquito netting into the brilliant sunshine. We discovered one another and drew together in an imaginary circle, putting death aside for a little longer and growing into one another before it was too late.

As my mother became weaker, I brought her the photo albums from New York so that she could identify the old pictures from Wappingers Falls. She was quick to point out a picture of me with her. I was holding my crotch and looking as if I were cornered, and she explained that people used to say I never got enough food when I was a kid. "They always thought I didn't feed you, you were so pale, but you never wanted to eat, you were such a nervous boy."

Most of the time she was peaceful and could drink only tea, and it wouldn't be long before she starved to death. But then the nursing home said it couldn't keep her any longer and that she would have to go back to Boston so she could be kept alive. There they'd put her on an i.v. to nourish her, and then of course, as the cancer spread, the real pain would begin. I said no, and the head nurse talked about God and said we shouldn't try to take God's place. I said we had to act as though there were a God and God knows God didn't want her to die in pain when all she was doing was dying in peace. But she was on the Massachusetts Old Age and there was nothing I could do. It was having no money again, not enough now even to keep my mother from the agony the state would impose upon her at the end.

I drove back to New York on Sunday night,

and she was to go to Boston on Tuesday. Before
I left her, we looked through the albums, and
she showed me a picture of Jim and Hattie
Clarke riding an enormous bicycle built for two
that he had built himself. Mother died the next
day, and, once again, it seemed in the nature of
things to put her in the Hawkins plot, another
handout from Uncle Dick, and no big deal.

When the time came to do something about
the graves, some twenty years later I regret to
say, I tried to have my mother and father moved
to the Chace burying ground in Swansea.
Everyone was buried there: the Senator; his
wife; the little children who had died in one
week of black diphtheria, their names engraved
on the bottom of a broken column that signified
the death of children; the Senator's father; his
father's father, and so forth. I figured the old
church graveyard had opened up more space in
the fields out back. But when I went to inquire
about reburying Holly and Mildred there, the
parish office said no, there was no more space
available, except of course on the lots where the
other Chaces already lay if there was any space
left at all; which meant, he continued, finding a
professional prober to poke away at the grassy
spots between the gravestones.

"But why dig them up at all?" my oldest
friend, the lawyer, asked. "Why not simply put

up a stone in the old Chace lot as though they were there? There's nothing left of them now, bones and dust, and the stone is simply to mark out their lives. Isn't that it?"

Which is what I did.

# Remember
# Pearl Harbor

For my parents the 1920s ended on Sunday morning, December 7th, 1941. Even with the Depression, even after Grandpa Clarke was thrown from the rumble seat in Columbia, South Carolina, Holly and Mildred went on drifting. The parties never stopped, and there were even out-of-season picnics in Poem Woods. It was a lovely day that first Sunday in December, the sky a lapis blue. Fall River with its three-decker tenements and its empty granite and brick mills seemed to brighten, though by 1941 it appeared to be in the last stages of a decay that would never be mended. The greatest cotton-spinning city in the world now had less than thirty operating factories.

Fall River itself was divided into three parts—the French-Canadians at the east end, familiarly known as the Flint; the Portuguese along the waterfront and the south end, known as the Globe; the Yankees and Irish sprawling over the northwest up from Main Street to the Highlands. We lived at the near peak of the hill where the high school, a granite clone of the Hôtel de Ville in Paris but with a Gothic spire and a red observatory, dominated even the massive tower of the print works. Living so close, I was late for school almost every day.

Where I grew up the streets were clean and shaded by elms and horse chestnut trees; but as you passed the city hall toward the Flint and the Globe, the streets were left untended, the trees were scant, and the neighborhoods were made up almost solely of tenements—gray and pink and brown with tiers of porches that sagged against their pillars. I remember in particular a park near the bar my father would visit while looking for votes for the next City Council election. Known as the Corky Row, the park was almost always empty. The swings were broken, the baseball batting cage shards of wire. If, running too fast, you tripped, your knees bled from the sharp stones of the playground. Before the war, then, the city seemed a desolate ruin made up of vast factory buildings, sprawling mansions and rows of tenements for the mill workers, who were largely the unemployed.

The Episcopal church that morning before

the Zeros struck was itself as quiet as death.
Sun came through in blue light above the altar.
I liked the tall gold cross I bore, and when I
unlocked it from its pew, I bowed without hy-
pocrisy before the altar. I took on the trappings
of priesthood: the gown of the crucifer billowed
about my body like the vestments of an arch-
bishop. To bear the cross was more to my style
than to serve as a mere choirboy, thin soprano
cracking into alto, and hardly able to read the
notes.

But the service itself seemed interminable:
I sympathized with those Puritans who had to
sit through hours of harangue. I, at least, could
listen to seventeenth-century prose from the
Book of Common Prayer, but even Mr. Cleveland's sermon, timed mercifully to last only
twenty minutes, came at one relentlessly. I buried comic books beneath the folds of my vestments and tried to read them between the open
pages of the hymnal while the old man was
speaking.

Tall, standing military-straight, he repeated in his sermons the lessons of the Great
War. For Mr. Cleveland, the irreducible fact of
his life was his year in the trenches of the Western Front. It wasn't the blood of the Lamb that
excited him, it was the blood spilled from
human entrails, the wastage of human life and
the necessity for heroism. The contradiction

seemed to stir the fires of the old theologian.
For him the overwhelming question wasn't how
could God allow the innocent to suffer and die,
but rather how could God permit heroism in
vain, man finding in his manner of dying rather
than in death itself his final justification for having lived? Like those aristocrats of the French
Revolution who achieved their finest hour on
the scaffold and on the firing line. Because, as
Mr. Cleveland once pointed out, the soldiers in
the Great War *had* died in vain. Wilson had
botched it, lurching off to Versailles and to the
mob. No wonder he was outfoxed, outgunned
and outmanned by the old tiger Clemenceau
and the Welsh witch Lloyd George. Europe was
a betrayal—all those lives lost in the swamp of
Europe, and their only monument an attitude
toward death. Heroism. Rebellion against the
human condition. Shaking their fists in God's
eye.

"Lord have mercy upon us. Christ have
mercy upon us"—his voice belted out the litany
—"that we should ever go to war again!" That
we should ever suffer the wounds of Europe,
that old sow, whose body *I* recognized years
later in Boston's Gardner Museum in Titian's
*Europa,* a prancing cow in a transport of lust.
Mr. Cleveland, then, though an Episcopalian,
was no friend of England, and through the fall
of 1941 warned us against God's wrath should

we take up arms in Europe's cause. He warned us against the sin of pride—Wilson's sin—that we should never presume to be God's messenger whose mission had come—in Wilson's words—"by no plan of our conceiving, but by the hand of God who led us in this way."

Pride was the deadliest sin, and for this we would be punished in ways passing our understanding. Let America expiate her own sins. And let him who is without sin cast the first stone. It would be criminal for us to set ourselves in judgment over any nation, even over Germany. And as for Japan? I doubt Mr. Cleveland held any opinion about Japan. Yellow and small, the Japanese lived only in the pages of missionary books, poor wretched of the earth to whom we allotted a portion of our mite boxes in Lent.

The service that morning was traditional, the season of Advent, my favorite time of the year. Not only was there the anticipation of Christmas with its promise this year of a cutdown pool table, but at church the celebrations were of seeming generosity: a creche for gifts for the poor, a Christmas party in the Gothic parish house, whose stairways led to secret places in the musty darkness, and the cadences of gospels that held me with their stories of heroism and rejection. The long journey of the Magi and the cruelty of innkeepers had made the miracle come true. Joseph did not complain, protected his wife, great with child, and, like my father, always the genial host, greeted those wise men bearing gifts. When the service ended, I would try to heed Mr. Cleveland's imprecations on the dangers of overweening pride while awaiting the glistening presents beneath the Christmas tree.

Prophetic the Book of Common Prayer that morning—"And there shall be signs in the sun, and in the moon, and in the stars; and upon the earth distress of nations, with perplexity; the sea and the waves roaring; men's hearts failing them for fear."

My father was waiting for me outside the church, and so I anticipated a treat. We would doubtless drive to Rhode Island where the bars opened early. I was only too content, at ten years old, to romance away the Sabbath with a short beer.

"James?" There was something in my father's voice that warned me.

"Hi."

"Hop in. We're not going home."

"Fine." En route to the bar we would surely stop at Clem Demo's for clam cakes.

"We're going to Aunt Ellen's. I don't want you home."

My father touched me on my shoulder. We had an almost physical need to be near one another. "You've got to stay at Ellen's for a bit," he said.

"What about lunch?"

"Lunch?" He paused; his hand squeezed the gear shift. "I really don't know. I guess there'll be something there."

We fell silent.

The car lurched up to the crest of the hill where the gabled houses of the millowners once stood, then beyond to the Historical Society and to the corner where my Aunt Ellen lived with her daughter, Lois, and Lucy, the black housekeeper, who must have been at least ninety then and treated all the Chaces with what seemed like controlled disdain. Ellen, beautiful at fifty-two, was my favorite aunt, and Shockie, her divorced husband, I adored. His basketball team in the 1920s was rumored to have beaten the original New York Celtics. For this alone I could have loved him.

But his heroic past was rivaled by the dangerous present. Shockie was a gambler. I heard tales of his daring at the racetrack and at roulette tables, for his divorce did not put him outside the family. I suspect, in fact, that he and Ellen simply got on better living apart. Something hung about him: the red Packard sedan, his gold cigarette lighter, his way with money, his flirtatious manner with my mother. When I ran into him on the corner he would often take me into the drugstore for a coffee milkshake, known in Fall River as a cabinet, and when it came time to pay the boy at the counter, Shockie simply opened his hand to reveal a palm filled with quarters and half-dollars; he would tell the boy to take what he wanted, though I saw his hand close over a boy's fist who dared to take too much. Shockie's power was real. To my Aunt Ellen as well as to me, he was a man who would brook no insults and stand up to a fight, and she would never really let him go.

The first words of my father when he ran up the steps to Ellen were: "Is Shockie here?"

"No."

"Where is he, then?"

"I think—at least, I hope—he's with Mildred."

"Good."

"Is Mother in trouble?" I asked.

"Sit down, Holly, and relax." My father fingered his moustache and did neither. "Hello, lover." Ellen put her arm around me: she wore four rings, and gold bracelets hung from her wrists. "What we've come to." She laughed.

My father turned away. "I'll make you a drink," he said.

"What are we going to do with you, Jimmy?" Ellen said.

"I don't know. And I don't like the question, either. What's wrong?"

"Pat broke her engagement to your brother."

All I can recall of Hollister in that time was something edgy in the way he laughed, something quick and too hard when he played with me. Like my brother, I, too, was a violent boy and became aware that something was dreadfully wrong—aware because I was told so— when I was about six. "You have St. Vitus' Dance," my mother explained. Whatever that actually meant, it called up for me the image of a marionette shaking and whirling. I was certainly wild, bouncing around my house, subject to uncontrollable rages that would give any parent a bad turn. How would I be described now —as a hyperkinetic child? In the 1930s, I was taken to the pediatrician who prescribed sunlamp treatments and rest periods, enforced each time by lying on a couch with a pillow under the small of my back.

By December 1941 I had grown calmer, in part because one day in the fifth grade I understood in a moment of sudden clarity that if I went on this way I would grow too strange for friendship. I made a calculated decision. I had to pretend to be one of the guys, and I was starting to do so just at that time, when my brother was probably at home less often after graduating from high school and knocking around at odd factory jobs while waiting to find a college that would take him. We were each in our separate ways trying to straighten out our lives. Though we slept in the same room from the day I was born, I date my vivid memory of him from that Pearl Harbor Sunday, when his violent behavior toward his girl friend threw the family into despair. Forever after, our relations were neither simply friendly nor simply distant: we were locked together in open conflict or in almost passionate love.

My father stared out the windows: the trees were covered with ice.

"I wish Shockie would get here," he said. "Jimmy, go to the kitchen and get a Coke."

As I left I heard him say to my aunt, "I hope Shockie's calmed Hollister down. The way he threatened Pat. It's a streak of violence I don't understand. And if I don't, you can imagine his mother's reaction."

"Let Shockie handle it. It's a blessing for Pat to be out of it. Hollister could have killed them both running the car up to ninety miles an hour just to make her take back that she didn't want to marry him after all."

"I wish I could get to him. But he gets so angry with me. I don't know why. Still, I can't give up on him."

"Shockie's better at dealing with him now-adays."

"I should be there."

As I came back with the bottle of soda, the door slammed.

"Your father's gone."

Ellen started to explain what had happened between Hollister and Pat, that Pat didn't want to commit herself to him when she was barely out of high school and the war was pending, and maybe she saw something too dangerous in him, the fire within that could break out to burn everything down around them. But Ellen knew nothing really of Hollister's fury, and probably wasn't much interested. Her obsession was with her own generation, with her own profound sense of loss. So, on a day when Hollister's crisis should have dominated her thinking, she began a monologue that, of course, I can't remember except the sense of it. She wandered about the small room as she spoke; she would touch my hair or squeeze my hand to make a point, and it was the story of the Chaces that I more or less knew anyway, from family dinners or from overheard conversations between my father and mother. But Ellen clearly believed that no matter who else had subjected me to this seductive history of the past, I should hear the tale from her, who alone knew how to tell it best. "When I was your age we had so much. And, Lord, it seemed we could do no wrong. The mills—if you could have seen them then—during the First World War, if the inventories were too large no one cared. It was produce, produce, and the cloth seemed to pile higher and higher. It was boom time. Things were so good, they even organized a conspiracy." I asked who *they* were, and Ellen explained that she meant the millowners. "You ought to know what the world is really like, Jimmy."

"But I *do* know."

"What I was saying is that during the war there was a conspiracy. The Europeans, before we got in, placed orders for millions of yards of bandage cloth in the United States. And most of the orders were sent to Fall River. But if the workers had known, they'd have demanded higher wages, and there'd have been less profits. So the millowners organized, secretly, a way of spreading the business among all the mills. Secret allotments. That way new orders wouldn't be quite so obvious. Oh, there was good business, everyone knew that, but to spread it out, to keep it going, that had to be done very carefully, very quietly. And so it was.

"Whenever a large order came through, they'd meet at night at home, to divide up the business. Quite the conspiracy, each of them coming and going separately, and the mill that got the order from Europe and couldn't handle it selling its share to another mill. That was how it was, Jimmy. Monstrous. And nothing set aside for after the war."

Conspiracy? It hardly seemed monstrous to me. But in her way she had explained to me the mean streets of my native city. Nothing put aside. A squandered life.

What I had always been told—or somehow believed I was told—was that the mills had been taken away by the South. It was the New England answer to the mythologies of the South —a way of life that somebody else had taken away. But that was not it at all. Conspiracies to conceal wealth. Low wages that forced strikes. Failure. Liquidations. Everybody got what he deserved. Or so, at least, Ellen seemed to be telling me. Theatrical, but the truth.

After her speech, I felt both exhilarated and frightened. I asked her if I could go home, and she said no, I should wait, she would give me a sandwich, and I should listen to the radio. Which I did. And heard the news of the bombing of Pearl Harbor.

Almost fifty years later the broadcast has invested itself with more drama than perhaps it had. There are those who believe they heard Winston Churchill call for blood, sweat and

tears, though it was shown later that the Prime
Minister had spoken those words in the House
of Commons, and they were not recorded. But
we knew: Aunt Ellen and I ran toward each
other; she cried out my name as though I were
the one that would be lost in the war; I twisted
in her arms with fear and excitement.

The news over the radio had to be shared.
Hollister, God save us, was old enough to fight.
Even Ellen forgot she was supposed to take care
of me. We would spread the news everywhere,
or at least from Walnut to Locust Street where
I lived. She held on to me to keep me from
slipping: there were slivers of ice on the pave-
ment, and we hurried along, sliding and lurching. In this driven, reckless manner we ran into
Hollister himself who, head bent into the wind,
bore down upon us.

"Did you hear the news?" we shouted.

Yes, yes, and he was going to enlist. To get
away from the awful mess this day had brought
him. He ranted against the Japanese. How
could they *do* it? And so we walked back to our
father and mother.

Hollister's hand was on my shoulder. The
clouds were feathery above us. It should have
been a gray, heavy day. But then, to enlist. To
ship out to sea. To feel liberated at last. Hollister straightened up and smiled; his hand on my
shoulder lost its weight as we swung along to-

gether, Ellen trailing behind. At that moment, we were in love.

Two months later: fog up from the river, a February morning, bitter dark and cold. I was awake early, with more than enough time to see my brother off at the station, but as I sat with my knees drawn up and shivering, I saw that the other twin bed was already empty. A splinter of light came from under the kitchen door; the Vulcan hot-water heater roared. The geography of that house where we lived before and during the war remains the most graphic landscape of my youth.

My grandmother's room was off the dining room and further walled off from us by the junk she had accumulated around the sewing machine. Mostly vestiges of Britain and Jim Clarke: a picture of the royal family, another of Jim's cricket team, his engraving tools, spools of thread and spindles. Across the dining room and off the living room was another bedroom where my parents slept. If I wanted to, I could press my ear to the wall and hear them talking late into the night. It was a house with many doors, extending the relatively restricted space; it also contributed to unexpected encounters when a door opened suddenly, for my father permitted no locks. For a child given to spying on grown-ups, it was a rich maze.

Even as I lay in my bed that February morning in 1942, I was aware of low voices from my mother's room. Almost instinctively I pressed my ear to the crack in the door. Hollister and my mother were talking, and she was apologizing. "I should have gotten up. I would have made you breakfast. You shouldn't go off like this."

"Mother, it doesn't matter."

"Haven't I always wanted you to go off on your own, never tried to hold you back? You used to run away, and I know, Hollister, I know what it's like to want to get out of Fall River, but you're so young—you *were* so young—and I didn't think it would be this way."

They fell silent. I imagined my mother with a dreamy smile falling back and turning into the pillow, and my brother looking away and turning abruptly, ready to bolt. It was only when the war was over that I knew about her drinking, when my father, standing again at the bedroom door with the kitchen light behind him, told me that he was helpless because she was helpless.

I waited for Hollister that cold February morning and listened to the quiet conversation that now came from behind the kitchen door. My father was saying, "You mustn't worry about your mother."

"Right."

"Leave it to me. I'll take care of her."

"Right."

The gutters dripped with last night's rain.

"I'm not really very hungry," Hollister said. "You think the war will be over soon?"

"Yes. And I wish you hadn't felt you had to enlist so quickly."

"Well, I didn't enlist just because I wanted to go to war."

"You didn't have to join the army if you just wanted to leave home, you know."

"I think I did."

"Hollister, no one could keep you here, even if we tried, even if we wanted to."

"Look," he said, "there wasn't any other way. I wanted to go someplace I can't run away from no matter how much I want to."

"I just wish you could have done it some other way."

"I would have been drafted anyway. Even in a short war. At my age."

"I suppose."

I was really cold now, and I felt something wrong hearing them this way. My brother was going off to war, he might be killed, and they were talking about something else. And then I knew I should stop thinking this and get my clothes on before it was too late to join them.

The white mist came up like fox fire as we drove to the train that would take the new re-

cruits to Fort Devens. I remember Hollister saying he couldn't even see the gold eagle on top of
City Hall, and my father had to put his head-
lights on low beam. The first shift at the mills
was just starting. You could hear the women in
the back yards taking in the milk bottles or
greeting the ice man. At one point I rolled down
the window to see if I could make out the red
brick of my school. "Funny I should almost lose
my way," my father said. "The fog's like soup."

There really was a high school band playing. My father said it reminded him of the First
World War. I didn't know what to say: something about it not taking so long to win this time
because trench warfare was obsolete and that
Hollister would write and would surely be
home for a while after basic training. Nobody
wanted to say goodbye, and nobody wanted to
cry. We almost stood around too long because
the train started up with a sudden lurch and
Hollister had to run for the steps. My father
held his hand so tightly that Hollister almost
lost his balance, and then we ran beside the
carriages until we saw him at the window rub-
bing the wet glass with his fist.

But it was the worst time of the war, and
Hollister never got home after basic. He was
eight weeks at Devens and then went to Fort
Bragg to learn fire direction control in the artil-
lery. He sent us a snapshot of himself standing

in formation with a gas mask on; then a month later in his shorts and dogtags among the sugar cane of Hawaii; and then there were no more pictures, just tiny scrawled V-mail letters. He was away for forty-two months and came back wounded and a hero.

When I left, twelve years later, from the Boston induction center, boarding a bus for Fort Dix, I believed what Hollister must have believed—that the army was a prison, but, paradoxically, only by literally turning myself in would I be free. In those days the Korean War, remote, without grace, had barely come to an end, and all of us would have to go into the army anyway. In the eight weeks before I was to go off to basic training, after a month in Fall River and then a month back in Cambridge during the last hot days of summer, when even the graduate students seemed to have migrated elsewhere, I was dry with fear, not of the army but of leaving home, of cutting myself off from parents and lovers, ready, so I believed in my foolishness, to let myself be killed to prove my terrible freedom. I threw myself into the army like a criminal.

On the way home from seeing Hollister off, my father held my hand. The high school band had stopped playing; the kids were buttoning mackinaws over their red and black uniforms.

The fog was lifting as the sun came over the hill; even the gold eagle of the city hall gleamed. But we were losing hold, I now know. My brother was gone, and his absence would remind my mother and father, year after year, that they had extended their youth beyond all bounds until, at Pearl Harbor, they found themselves suddenly both grown up and growing old.

I don't know what it was like for my brother his first morning at Fort Devens away from us at last. But I remember at Fort Dix the sun rising against a harvest moon, and the New Jersey plain like a moonscape. My brother and I were the first explorers.

# Partisans

I remember a picture of an old woman dragging a cart. It must have appeared in *Life* magazine during the Spanish Civil War, and she became for me the archetype of all the refugees from wars that I have seen or known. Why I should recall this photograph taken when I was seven or eight years old is simply beyond me, unless it was because of my grandmother, Hattie Clarke, who bore herself like a displaced person. All the other pictures ran counter to the image of the Spanish peasant, for the 1940s were a time when heroes were abundant. They came not only in movies but most often on bubblegum cards, their faces streaked with blood and dust, and I was good at winning them from my classmates by pitching them against the cement wall of the schoolyard at recess. Whoever pitched his card closest to the wall picked up the lot. At first they showed scenes from World War I, barbed-wire and exploding mines and men in saucer-brimmed helmets at the ready going over the top with rifles cradled; later, after the Battle of Midway, P-38s divebombing a Japanese warship. Violence everywhere. Willed violence. The violence of children and the celebration of violence, which became more acute as we convinced ourselves that the war was going to affect us as it had France and England. How we longed for heroism.

Pearl Harbor was shown again and again on Movietone news reels—or so it seemed. At first all the news was bad. The Bataan death march, Corregidor, Singapore—we got V-mail from Hollister that told us nothing. In a bay window we hung a small flag with a simple blue star on it to show that my brother was in the army. But it wasn't a gold star. Not yet. He wasn't dead. Not yet. All I knew was, he was on the way to being a hero.

My father, as he himself pointed out, had fought only "the battle of College Hill" at Holy Cross during the First World War. But now he was appointed district air raid warden for Fall River. Forcing people to turn out the lights or pull the shades lent him an inappropriate authoritative air. Our house was filled with war materiel: pamphlets on gas warfare, great white helmets, gas masks, spades, boots and jackets,

flares, first-aid kits, and the leviathan of our
arsenal—a civil defense fire extinguisher. It
was an oversized can with a pump handle, but
when it was filled with water and pumped hard,
its nose discharged a violent spray so concen-
trated it could knock a man over if he were
taken unawares. Our equipment was stored in
the cellar—which was also our air-raid shelter,
my clubhouse and sometimes a laboratory.
(When I was younger I had followed the in-
structions of Tom Swift's diamond-makers but,
without a mountaintop in the Andes or a proper
lightning rod, I failed.)

In those days we waited for the air raids. I
memorized German fighter planes—those
black silhouettes of a Messerschmidt 110 or a
Fokker 140—and spent early mornings shivering on top of the Flatiron Building before I had
to go to school. Beyond the mills, on the edge of
the city where the urban landscape fell away
and the woods began, I could see the reservoir.
Large fir trees, birches, scrub oak over which
no planes came. A year before, on the eve of the
war when I was ten years old, I had fled those
woods as trees burned all about me. We had
gone into the reservoir to escape. A friend had
plotted out exactly where a clearing should go.
To this day I have no idea if what happened was
really an accident, for it seems hard to believe
that we were so naive. He touched a match to

dry leaves, and the wind, up from the reservoir, caught the flames. A bush burned. And another. The saplings flamed like tinder. The spreading was too quick. All the leaves and trees burned, and by the time we ran away, the bark of the trees was aflame.

By the second year of the war, though the artifacts of battles became commonplace, the threat of invasion and divebombing had faded. We were forced to invent danger. So, at night, on a summer's evening at our cabin in Tiverton, Rhode Island, I would pole my skiff away from the shore, dipping my oar into the water as silently as I imagined the enemy might do. The parties from before the war had all but stopped; lights went out earlier now in the cottages on the shore, and my parents went to bed earlier. My mother, who had never worked and who had stopped driving after one not serious accident in 1936, had started running a dry-cleaning shop. She repeatedly praised herself for beginning work at forty-three. And I can understand now the courage it took. Unlike me, she never acted out of bravado; like goosepimples her fear—and her courage—showed through.

In the cellar the air raid equipment grew dusty. My father's rounds at night, flashing his light at those whose blackout curtains were hanging loose, became less frequent, then ended with the end of summer. The Nazis must have known we were finally invulnerable. The short nights of late summer, when sunset came at eight, dispelled the fear of air raids. By fall I came back to a city possessed, I believed, by subversion. If the planes were not to come through, then there must be something else in the air. I soon formed a club called the Partisans, named for the guerrillas in Yugoslavia who fought in roving bands, hit-and-run and run again, against the Nazis. Paramilitary in its organization, the club met in my cellar, which was stocked with handbooks on defense against gas warfare. The cellar made an excellent underground bunker. Those of us who formed the nucleus of the club gathered together every afternoon to train ourselves as commandos. Partisans of a war that had not come, we were urban guerrillas ready to fight off the invaders while gathering information on the fifth column.

The group itself was hardly a match even for a gang of toughs from another neighborhood. Jimmy Kay, who seemed more at home making marionettes than conducting group warfare, had originally founded a three-man commando unit, but he had been willingly replaced through a coup I had organized when I wanted to absorb his unit into the Partisans. His participation after that was occasional, and

he spent much of the time belittling our efforts
at surveillance and counterespionage. The du-
tiful Jimmy McAdams, whose temper flared un-
expectedly when he suddenly realized he was
being taken for granted, and Bobby Kean, an
amiable, lumbering fellow whose scientific bent
lent him a special authority on gas warfare,
completed the cadre.

Most of the work consisted of learning pas-
sages from training manuals from my father's
civil defense work or studying remote theaters
of operation on National Geographic maps. Ex-
aminations were rigorous, marking severe,
punishments merciless. Deviation was scarcely
permitted; no explanations were accepted. Pun-
ishment was an isolation cell in my cellar, and
readmittance was gained by admitting error
and agreeing to carry out orders. Only occa-
sionally did the group carry its activities outside the basement rooms. It seemed to us far
less significant to apprehend a spy (who, in any
case, proved as elusive as the Scarlet Pimper-
nel) than to gather data about espionage. Hours
were spent making up the cartography of ten
city blocks; diagrams of the houses—their lay-
outs and approaches—were traced with archi-
tectural care. Later, we fortified the basement
rooms. We laid traps; it became a veritable
workshop of counterespionage. By using pul-
leys, we raised baskets of ashes over the pipes;

then we drilled holes in the walls, through
which the nozzle of a hose was fixed like the
barrel of a gun. At the far end, the very prefig-
urement of a bunker, was the room that contained the charts and manuals of the Partisans.
We kept them like treasure, for the way was
closely guarded and entrance gained at the peril
of falling into a cistern.

Violence became a way out of boredom.
After the maps and the nomenclature of gases
were thoroughly memorized, homework for its
own sake became untenable. We would test the
defenses of the bunker ourselves, so that to survive the traps—which could not in any case be
avoided—became some final proof of manhood.
It was also understood without ever being made
explicit that the final redoubt, like a fort along
the Maginot Line, could never be invaded: at
best the enemy would be able to mount an as-
sault.

The end came on a listless afternoon. We
had found a new recruit—Herbie Rosenthal—
who seemed eager to be accepted but who was,
unlike us, a ruffian, with baying laughter and
rough, unexpected embraces. Stung with hu-
miliation, dripping with ashes, he somehow
bulled his way to the last door and howling with
fury, banging and shoving against the latch,
tore away at our last defenses, and so broke
inward. Then, as we had known must happen,

he fell through the open trapdoor into the final
trap, a cistern.

His leg was badly hurt, and he had to be
helped home. Though he recovered, it was all
too dangerous, too violent. We were terrified of
what we had done—here, after all, was a guy
we knew, not the invader we had so long prayed
for.

It may have been about that time, during
the first American landings in the Pacific, that
my brother wrote of killing his best friend in
the night. He gave no details; the sentence itself
was broken off—"I couldn't see. . . ."

What had happened? Lost in the night?
Stumbling for a latrine? And my brother, gun
cocked, the hand too quick on the trigger for
the enemy in the blackness? The Japanese,
whom he had not seen, remained hidden in the
forest until they attacked, and his whole company died. Hollister survived behind the accidental shield of a coconut log and received the
Purple Heart and the Bronze Star.

We disbanded the Partisans soon after
Herbie's accident. Though it was no one's fault,
we had to end it. By 1944 the war was almost
commonplace. At the point where news is no
news at all. And politics, for a while, became
irrelevant. But politics in Fall River was not
something one could easily get away from. For

it was politics built on favors owed and paid
back. Almost no one I knew had much hope of
making it except by escaping to another city, or
by finding an angle at home that would give you
a bare living. The prerequisites of office meant
work for an alcoholic brother-in-law, or a summer job on construction for a nephew at B.U.
After all, here was a city that had literally de-
clared bankruptcy during the Depression,
whose finances for years had to be approved by
a board chosen by the state, and no meager
wartime boom was about to restore it. To be
called a con man was a kind of compliment.
Though even con men could be outsmarted.

"Listen, James—" My cousin still lectures
me in the same tough tone of voice. "Don't kid
yourself. You've got to find an angle to survive."
Finding an angle, however, meant staying in
Fall River. If, as I was by high school, you were
scheming to get out, politics, particularly of the
Massachusetts kind, was something to avoid.
The low politics of Fall River, squalor and failure, meant cracks about the French and the
Irish and the Portuguese, while far away in
Washington, or on battleships in the Atlantic,
or in the cool white villas of Casablanca, F.D.R.
consorted with Churchill and de Gaulle.

Eventually I did escape, and to a place
where politics—high or low—was all but absurd. The generation that had returned to Har-

vard College at the end of World War II had
known the desperate value of politics—something we did not know; and so to have entered
Harvard in 1949, as I did, was to discover a
world where politics was fast becoming irrelevant. The flickering beginnings of the cold war
left us with few illusions that the good war,
which had just been fought and whose veterans
were now graduating, was to lead to a better
world of equity and justice. We turned away
from politics with the implacable vengeance of
the young. Dimly we learned of the Communist
coup in Czechoslovakia and the Berlin blockade, and it seemed as though the uneasy peace
that now prevailed left no room for young romantics, in either politics or art. Of course we
were romantics, possessed, as the young usually are, by what Paul Valéry once called the
fever of reason; but we would go into battle as
anti-romantics, banishing the self into some
higher order over which thought would linger
and love play.

Nor did going to Harvard truly mean
breaking away. I had only too carefully cultivated a circle of friends in high school, and two
of them went along with me for my freshman
year. If I was to learn to stand on my own, I
should have begun earlier; instead, it was not
until I returned from Paris years later that I

threw myself into the army before it was too late to grow up.

There were three decisive moments when I refused to grow up: the first, at ten or so, concerned the idea of going off to camp, something I, not my parents, had seized on. I don't think I thought about what lay in store: it was an abstract decision. But on the day I was to leave, I was overcome with terror. What did I think the camp counsellors would do to us? And why did I imagine I wouldn't survive? I don't suppose my parents could have actually dispatched me to camp. With me refusing to go, what were they to do? There was an edgy danger in my tantrum. My parents, careless, undemanding, gave in.

Refusing to go to boarding school five years later was much easier. No one insisted, after all. And I could find good reasons for turning down the scholarship to Saint Mark's School. Convinced by Jimmy McAdams, who had been sent off to military school, that the restrictions were cruel and arbitrary, I shrugged off that journey. Was I not already finding a place for myself at the high school? And even a starting position as a forward on the church basketball team, and regular attendance at the Saturday night dance? But once again, the real reason was fear of someplace else.

A third time, I truly thought I would break away. But unlike the other opportunities, my imagination failed me. The end of my freshman year at college I agreed to take a job as a waiter in Maine. My father tried, dimly, to warn me against it. He took me on a nostalgic ride to Island Park for a hot cheese and a beer. He was looking worried most of the time, about money I think now, but he said nothing. "You won't like it," he said, and ordered me another beer. Neither of my parents complained. Was it their way of keeping me to themselves? I don't think so. I had already been living away a year. Perhaps he just sensed that I was again operating on bravado. Or perhaps he remembered the other failures of separation better than I did. Or remembered the week-long agony when I tried to hold a job in a cotton mill: I was just fourteen and found the cotton lint clogging my throat and nose and the noise of a hundred looms too much to take. But I had held other jobs since then. Working in an inn in Maine would not be so different from what I had done summers in Tiverton, which was, however, only a twenty-minute bus ride away. As the train pulled away from the Providence station, my parents neither encouraged nor stopped me. Just the cloudy questioning eyes of my father. "Are you sure, Jimmy?"

It was late that night that the panic came:

in the small attic room I was assigned to, lying under the eaves, I hardly slept. Maine was a foreign country, after all. And the next day, in the empty hotel through the bank of windows of the dining room shone a cold thin sun, and the emptiness.

I bolted. Some excuse about my parents being sick. Escape seemed the only alternative, and I knew my father would post bail for me. Still, the return home was a failure that I couldn't dodge, no matter how artful. No one, however, was even disappointed in me; nor was there the hint of a reproach. Nothing was ever to be held against me. I was always being given a clean slate.

The price paid was to go into the cotton mills, working at a machine that stripped bobbins of their remaining threads. The roar of the loom never left my head. But as the weeks passed, I learned how comforting was the routine of an eight-hour shift, how the mind, habituated to the simplest tasks, becomes free. I learned how easy it is to prefer unhappiness to simple risk. It would be four more years before I could even begin to understand that the known landscape must be abandoned again and again and again.

I must have been assigned the smallest suite imaginable in an obscure corner of Har-

vard Yard—a living room with four desks, two
bedrooms with double-decker bunks, and a
bathroom in the shape of a narrow broomcloset.
I met each of my three roommates with apprehension: the first to appear was Lennie, a sham-
bling midwesterner from a Chicago private
school whose rather gentle manners presided
over the tensions of that year with remarkable
decency. As upperclassmen we never saw each
other.

The second one to arrive was Dick, who,
though he stayed with us throughout the aca-
demic year, held himself apart. He was from a
small town in Maine, and in the confusion of
Harvard College, found a passion in fencing, so
much so that he slept with his epee. Sometime
during his sophomore year, I believe, he quietly
left the college.

The last roommate to arrive was Michael
Peirce. His appearance, as I remember it, star-
tled me, for he showed up at the doorway
stripped to his boxer shorts and carrying bar-
bells. Since the only unoccupied bunk was the
one above mine, he had to choose it. Michael's
father, Waldo Peirce, was a painter in the manner of Renoir fifty years too late, whose deliberately bohemian life had left Michael to fend
for himself through a succession of boarding
schools. His father had driven an ambulance on
the Western Front during the First World War,

run bulls with Hemingway, and returned to
Maine and Key West during the Depression.
Michael tried to bear the weight of his father
easily, but he was obsessed with him and under
constant pressure to respond with love. Post-
cards came two or three times a week, scraps
of advice or information accompanied by a
drawing or watercolor. Like his father, Michael
wore his hair uncombed, a stained tweed
jacket, tennis shoes and chino pants. He let me
organize his social life, make friends for him
and, despite his imposing figure, was gentle to
me and to all of us. It was as if he were bewildered at having survived the coarse, imposing
father, to say nothing of the apparently uncar-
ing mother he barely knew but with whose craziness—real and feigned—he refused to deal.
His connection through his father to the larger
world of Paris between the wars lent him a mys-
terious presence that enthralled me.

The first year seemed to have no shape. I
talked literature and coxed the freshman crew.
Harvard College at the time was two-thirds
prep-school graduates and derived its tone
from them. I soon discarded my long-roll la-
pelled, double-breasted suit for a severe, three-
button Oxford grey flannel. That was the easy
part. More complicated was to take on the air
of assertiveness that was never more apparent
than among the oarsmen of the freshman crew.

They all seemed to have gone to boarding schools (though I later discovered that some of the best rowers came from public high schools in the Midwest and had never touched an oar before), and they seemed at ease with themselves. It was not cockiness but a kind of nerveless manner that was both intimidating and oddly reassuring. They were also enormous: long arms and long legs and broad shoulders (no wonder Harvard won crew races and lost football games, their best athletes were on the crew) and I, a sliver of a boy, was absolutely scrawny by comparison. As coxswain, of course, I was supposed to shout orders and keep the count.

When we won the first race of the spring, I was so stunned that I forgot where the finish line was and kept the boat going, my crew, like galley slaves, obedient to my order until the coach cried out from the launch to stop. For failing to know where the finish was, I lost my place as varsity cox.

The final disaster came on a soft May afternoon when I was practicing with the second-string heavies and failed to see a single scull oarsman in a wherry under an arching red-brick bridge. At the last moment, just as eight huge oarsmen in the shell I was coxing—their backs to the wherry—were about to come down on the unwitting sculler, the coach surely saved his life by shouting, "Starboard oars up." I was removed as cox, banned to the launch, and given a stopwatch as a timer. Whatever was I doing there, anyway?

I don't know now whatever possessed me to believe my family could afford Harvard. I must have assumed that scholarships would rain down on me, but I received none. Peter Collias, on the other hand, my closest friend in high school, had won a national scholarship to Harvard because, in fact, he was a better scholar than I, as well as an athlete who played championship basketball with demonic energy. Moreover, it was he who had persuaded me to apply there. My father, when I told him I was applying to Harvard, simply and justly asked how I was planning to pay for it. He suggested Brown, so I could commute, and like Mr. Micawber, I replied, something will turn up. Which it did.

Jim McAdams, sometime Partisan, sullen at military school but always the loyal friend on vacation, must have told his mother of my plight. The whole story came out later, after I'd graduated: it seemed McAdams' mother had asked some of her friends who were Harvard graduates what they were going to do for "one of their own" who could not afford to go to the college. They had apparently never been confronted with that kind of situation before, since their own, unlike the Portuguese or French, never seemed to need a scholarship. But the answer was quite clear—send the Chace boy to Harvard. And so they did, raising a special fund through the Harvard Club just for me. Which is how I found myself walking back to the Yard with a stopwatch in my hand, as eight-oared shells I no longer coxed slipped under the Eliot Bridge on their way to the willowy reaches of the river beyond Watertown.

In my freshman year I also joined the literary magazine, *The Harvard Advocate*. Its quarters then rested above Benny Jacobson's Valeteria in a series of rundown offices, including a gloomy sanctum for our weekly board meetings. There, gathered around a twelve-foot oak desk, beneath the wooden plaques inscribed with the names of past board members, among them famous novelists and poets, we acidly deliberated the fate of undergraduate prose and poetry. Once again, I found myself on the awkward edge of things. Just after the war the *Advocate* was dominated by critics and poets who talked as though they were too weary to be bothered with the things of this world and seemed perpetually high on cigarettes. But of course they graduated, and by 1951 the literary tone changed. Our new board was determined to promote the work of undergraduates and to confine all literary criticism to the pages of the

book-review section. Entrepreneurs of literature, we ran contests, sponsored public read-
ings, and enticed T.S. Eliot and Dylan Thomas
to donate their proceeds to the magazine. Besides Eliot, who not only dominated the New
Critics but whose visits to Cambridge—and the
*Advocate*—imposed on him even more authority, the pantheon included Pound, Yeats, Vir-
ginia Woolf, Conrad, Ford Madox Ford, D.H.
Lawrence and Scott Fitzgerald. Over their more
immediate influences brooded the triumvirate
of Proust, Joyce and Mann, who were read vir-
tually in their entirety by students in Harry
Levin's one-semester course by that same
name; it seemed impossible for us to free ourselves from their collective ghosts. Unlike
Pound, who knew the answer to the question
Where Do You Go After Swinburne, the undergraduate poets did not know where to go after
Yeats.

How hard it was to rebel in Cambridge,
when what I and my friends believed in was
now blessed. Intellectuals from small towns,
loners from boarding schools, the whole pano-
ply of malcontents irritated beyond measure at
the ordinary society they confronted that was
too preoccupied to pay attention to them, found
themselves enclosed in an accepting world. The
biggest turnout that I can recall was for T.S.
Eliot, who came to read from the *Four Quartets:*

"And so each venture / Is a new beginning, a raid on the inarticulate / With shabby equipment always deteriorating / In the general mess of the imprecision of feeling, / Undisciplined squads of emotion. And what is there to conquer / By strength and submission, has already been discovered / Once or twice, or several times, by men whom one cannot hope / To emulate. . . ."

We listened to Eliot and were overwhelmed with fatigue. We seemed to lust, at times, for middle age—perhaps because we were so frustrated in our youth. Our longings could be fulfilled only with age, when fame or failure—for we admitted no middle ground—would then be decided. If there was an unarticulated idea, it was to not be concerned with public issues—foreign or domestic—but rather to work out as best you could your own integrity.

Among literary folk there was talk of a protest against the imprisonment in a mental hospital of Ezra Pound. No one questioned that he was guilty of treason, but we felt he had been punished enough by the cage of Pisa. "Pull down thy vanity," he had written—and so the world had. Nothing came of it. Archibald MacLeish and Ernest Hemingway and Robert Frost secured his release while we undergraduates risked nothing. We were not indifferent to politics, we were positively hostile to it. Politics, particularly social politics, was a cop-out, not so much the annihilation as the loss of self.

Haunted as we were by the great literary figures of the past we sought solace in the stars. Specifically, we decided, with a sinking sense of bravado, we would get in touch, Ouija-like, with the ghosts of literature past. Yeats was the obvious candidate—the old theosophist, turning in his gyres, was surely ready to reach down to us, all the more so since he, more than most poets, understood our sexuality. Did he not cry out in his old age—"Go your ways, O go your ways, / I choose another mark, / Girls down on the seashore / Who understand the dark."

But there were other candidates to appeal to, the more awesome the better. Unfortunately, neither our French nor our German was much good; therefore, no Proust and no Mann. Indeed, the medium—for that is what we sought—would doubtless speak only English. This argued for an American, someone who would find it amusing to speak to half a dozen undergraduates who resisted the future like Luddites. We followed, as one of us put it, the beat of an antique drum. It was therefore decided that we would find a psychic to get in touch with Gertrude Stein—Hemingway's

tutor, Picasso's madonna, the mother of us all
—who would speak to our condition at a seance
in Chelsea, Massachusetts.

Two colleagues from the *Advocate,* Harvey
Ginsberg and George Kelly, drove over the
Mystic River Bridge with me for a rendezvous
with the Reverend Lilla Shay. In streets as familiar as my own Fall River, people bent over
against the cold; the car slid across the gray
snow and ice. George had already haunted the
streets of Boston behind Symphony Hall until
he found a temple of theosophists, and there,
wrapped in a woolen turban embroidered with
galaxies, was the Reverend Lilla Shay. "Gertrude Stein?" she said. "Then you must be from
Harvard. *She* went to Radcliffe, you know. That
is what I know about Gertrude Stein." It was
that last, Stein-like line that persuaded George
that Lilla was our blithe spirit. Since Lilla lived
in Chelsea, to Chelsea then we went, wired
for the spheres, without even a drink to fortify
us.

"Better all the Detroit factories be de-
stroyed than one El Greco," I said gravely.

"Ah, Chace, your problem is"—we halted
before the three-tiered brown tenement and
stamped up the snowy steps. George, popeyed
and self-deprecating, squinted through light
horn-rimmed glasses and suppressed a laugh—
"you like El Greco. But everything looks too

much the same in El Greco. Surely you can do better than that." (Years later, I found I did not, in fact, much like El Greco, and even wrote a book explaining why the Detroit factories ought to be saved.)

On the second-floor landing, the Reverend Lilla Shay greeted us with an arm extended in an invitation to a seance. "Sir Niles appears ready," she said, as we settled ourselves in the parlor, sinking into overstuffed chairs covered in chintz and antimacassars. "I think we will be successful tonight."

"May we make a contribution?" Harvey said. He was a polite boy from Bangor, Maine, the president of the *Advocate,* and ridden with compulsions. He was fanatically devoted to the novels of William Faulkner, and as president published an issue of the *Advocate* with critical articles on Faulkner, with a cover drawing by Waldo Peirce. We have lunched together at least once a month for over thirty years.

"Not now."

"Shall we turn off the lights?" George asked.

"Why in Heaven's name would you want to do that?" She scrutinized us for any trace of mockery. "The lights are quite low enough."

And they were. Dim under tasseled shades. A tinkling of bells in the distance. It seemed to grow somewhat darker.

"Sir Niles? These gentlemen. Do you hear me, Sir Niles?"

A tinkling of bells. An automobile horn in the far streets. The Reverend Lilla Shay closed her eyes and leaned forward in the easy chair. "Do not escape me. Do not bolt."

Silence. No one breathed.

"Lilla? Lilla Shay?" The voice, a little shaky, came through, nonetheless, loud and clear.

"For God's sake!" The Reverend Lilla Shay sprang from the chair and pushed open the door to the kitchen. "Arthur, not now," she cried. "Can't you wait for supper? Must your needs always come first? Eat and die? Is that it? Is that all there is?"

There was more silence. George poured himself a jigger of sherry from the decanter on the buffet and downed it in a gulp.

Lilla Shay returned, and the seance continued. But Sir Niles was recalcitrant now. "Come back, Sir Niles." We waited. I wanted to bail out. Lilla Shay smiled. "He is coming back." She paused. "He is here." She turned to George. "Your contribution, please."

"You'll take a check?"

"Is it a Massachusetts bank?"

"It is."

"Leave it there on the buffet next to the

sherry you've been drinking." She looked at me and then at Harvey. "Ready on the left? Ready on the right?"

"Ready on the firing line," Harvey said, absolutely serious.

"Gertrude Stein. Gertrude Stein. Gertrude Stein."

The silence of the spheres. Then Lilla Shay smiled with contentment.

"She is here."

"Will she tell us where we are?" I asked.

"Where you are?"

"Where we are."

"You are in Chelsea, Mass. That is where you are. Why should she tell you what you already know?"

"No, I mean where we are and where we are going."

"Yes, there," Harvey said. "Miss Stein will understand."

The Reverend Lilla Shay nodded. She swayed in her chair while rocking forward as though to faint, and the tassels on the lamps moved. "There." Very softly.

"What?" George asked. The tassels moved.

And then, with a howl, the Reverend Lilla Shay threw back her head and uttered Gertrude Stein's immortal warning: "There is no there there."

With that, we paid up, lost our way four
times driving back to Cambridge, and drank
whiskey until dawn.

Whiskey and martinis were our addictions.
No one took drugs. I knew about heroin because Billie Holiday had got hooked and was
put in prison for it; otherwise, drugs came out
of literature—opium out of Coleridge and Coc-
teau, cocaine out of Cole Porter ("Some get a
kick from cocaine / I'm sure that if I took even
one sniff / That would bore me terrific'ly, too /
Yet I get a kick out of you")—and marijuana
was smoked by jazz musicians and known as
reefers. Yet a number of us took drugs at Harvard—not because we were much interested in
them, but because we were paid to do so. It was
easy money, and I guess we thought it was
harmless because the drugs were shot into our
veins by medical doctors at two of Boston's
leading hospitals. Word got around that you
could make five bucks an hour, better pay than
typing other kids' papers, and if the reaction
wasn't too severe, you could even get in a little
studying as you lay on the hospital cot for the
three hours you went under.

The doctors never told me what drugs I
would be injected with; as I recall they were
mind-altering drugs like mescaline, and heroin
I believe, and of course placebos. It was done

in a series to see if there was a psychological disposition as to how the drugs affected us. So there were Rorschach tests and multiple choice, given before and during the experiments. Docile and cooperative, we shrugged off the occasional, mild nausea that sometimes afflicted us. Alone in the hospital room, generally bored and only mildly disoriented, I tried without much success to read a textbook on the French Revolution. But at one session, without warning, the bleak hospital room seemed to me as perfectly in balance as a Cézanne painting.

The worst and final session I had was taking LSD, or lysergic acid, as it was then called. We knew it would be a rough day because the pay was a princely twenty-five dollars an hour. It was supposed to induce psychotic symptoms similar to those of schizophrenia. This time the door was locked, I was observed through a window, and this time I went truly mad. I cursed and broke a chair and was convinced that something had gone dreadfully wrong, that the doctors had made a mistake and the dosage was too high and I would never come out of it. My roommate, Michael Peirce, told me he went into a near catatonic state. It was only then that we saw we were using our bodies far too carelessly, and we called it quits.

•   •

Cambridge at the time had not yet at-
tracted so many psychiatrists, and the rents off
Brattle Street were reasonable. The shops were
hardly chic; restaurants featured whale steak,
or worse. Shabby genteel. During the school
year the bounds of Cambridge itself were very
much those of the university. The world of Brattle Street, of large houses and closed gardens
that swing about the Yard like a crescent, fad-
ing out somewhere beyond the Divinity School
—this world I knew much better years later
when I visited my in-laws and witnessed the
tensions of middle-aged teachers and lawyers
who had lived too long among the young. Far
from being an Arcadia, Cambridge later seemed
a confining world whose center was Harvard;
those who were excluded from this metropole
ached to be a part of it.

This same world flourished in the summers. In my junior year I decided to remain in
Cambridge and find a summer job. How the city
festered in the July heat; students and their
girls—admitted easily to the dorms during
summer school—sprawled on the grass,
perched on the Buddha idol next to Widener
Library, slept in one another's arms along the
river bank. Because I was working in the Yard
itself, uncomprehendingly copying out a trans-
literation of Sino-Mongolian tablets at the
Yenching Institute, I met older men and

women, graduate students who now taught
elsewhere but who returned in the summer to
work on their still-unfinished theses.

Cambridge became an island, and in the
long evenings there was often violence in the
air. But it was a Jamesian violence, private
moral crises that stropped on one's nerves like
a razor. After serving in the Second World War
these graduate students had come back to as-
sert a vision of a world that had disappeared.
They rejected the quick marriages that followed
the war, the rush to the suburbs, the efforts to
construct a world safe from the Depression.
What was starting to wear them away, as I only
dimly understood, was their perception of a future that would make it impossible to recapture
time lost. Savage parties, foolish drinking, were
reflections of what they imagined was the life of
the 1920s, as was the return to Paris, running
with the bulls in Pamplona, the escape into
drugs in Greenwich Village, and then back to
Cambridge to try to figure out what was going
wrong and maybe put in some time in graduate
school. And so they lunged about, searching for
sexual connections so callously that they made
licit our own longings to break out of the still
formal pattern of our courtships. Or so it
seemed to me—for the sexual advances appeared indiscriminate in the sultry gardens off
Brattle Street.

Looking back on the period that was then ending, Lucy Edwards, who is now an editor at *Foreign Affairs,* has written of the generation that had just returned from the war to the university and that corresponded, she felt, to the one Scott Fitzgerald described in his stories of the jazz age: "Now as then, youth, money, and fame seemed in infinite supply, for those who could help themselves to them. Everybody was reading Scott Fitzgerald whose books, out of print in the '30s and early '40s, were being rapidly reissued." Heirs to a tradition, "we saw ourselves, our parties, our clothes, our conversation through a Fitzgeraldian haze." But like the phony war of 1939, it proved to be a phony jazz age. By the Korean War, it was all over. The new "romantic profession" became the CIA. The cold war was as inevitable as middle age.

Some of us went into the army reserves in order to postpone the draft. Harvey Ginsberg, Michael Peirce and I—an unlikely three soldiers—pulled out our uniforms on Wednesday nights and studied fire-direction control in a warehouse classroom. But the summer of our junior year also meant two weeks of summer camp, and for the first time we began to understand that being in the army meant going a long way away.

The train to Camp Drum, Watertown, New

York, was hot and dusty in midsummer, and despite the weekly drills, we were woefully unprepared. All the NCOs were tougher than those we encountered in the regular army, three years later. But after all, it was only two weeks, and there was no time to become used to becoming a soldier. We didn't even anticipate a bad time. We loaded howitzers and lobbed shells into the middle distance. Michael shut up and read *Othello* under a tree. Harvey crawled crabwise through the dust, while trying to light a cigarette. I don't think he expected he'd make it even fifty yards under the barbed wire. War games. What did Camp Drum have to do with Korea? Upon returning to Cambridge Harvey, Michael and I sat again in leafy gardens and talked about anything but politics.

The last year the aesthetic tone of Cambridge grew pervasive. Jacobean tragedies of blood were performed in a theater in an alley. Dylan Thomas, fat and flushed, in America to make money by declaiming his poems, lurched through an *Advocate* party, driven toward an early grave by drink and undergraduates. At the Thomas party everything turned into shambles: Harvey was smashed in the nose by Charles Neuhauser, the most uncompromising member of the editorial board, while the Welsh poet pawed Charles's girl. Harvey, George Kelly, Peter Collias and I left for New York at

midnight, only to discover somewhere outside
New Haven that we had but twelve dollars
among us. We never made it to New York and
drove slowly back to Cambridge the next day,
taking a long circuitous route in the late fall
afternoon to Hyannisport where George spent
his summers. Everything was pale green and
pale gray, eelgrass along the beaches, and the
sky so clear and blue you could believe you saw
the Vineyard and beyond where the Azores lay.
A larky day with not much to talk about, feeling
vaguely guilty about plying Dylan Thomas with
so much drink that the *Advocate* party had
turned into a drunken brawl.

   T.S. Eliot's visit was another matter—more
successful and seemingly characteristic of the
man. He had come a year earlier to deliver the
lecture that had drawn the largest audience
ever, and there had been a reception. But the
celebrity was cornered like an animal, about to
be assaulted by graduate students. This year,
on a private visit to a cousin, he accepted our
invitation to meet for tea with no more than a
half dozen or so undergraduates. (Charles said,
"I really have nothing to say to Eliot." Later he
would startle his senior board of examiners.
Upon being asked whom one should start with
in a study of twentieth-century poetry he
snapped, "Robert Lowell." Poor Charles, he
should never have gone to Harvard. A brilliant,

hard-edged Jewish boy from a New York City
high school, Charles was forever embarrassed
by his background and feigned a patrician up-
bringing. He finally joined the CIA, refused to
suffer fools gladly, and implied that he was a
man who could keep secrets; he also made it
clear that he believed what outsiders presumed
to know about foreign affairs was both irrelevant and absurd. He never liked any poets after
Lowell or music after Beethoven or painting
after Turner.) For an hour or so Eliot sat and
talked about a proposed screenplay of *Murder
in the Cathedral*; the air was heavy with dust in
the late afternoon sunlight. Eliot was gentle
with us, and when he left he seemed bent but
dogged as he went down the stairs into the
slushy streets, the Prufrockian image intact.
Like Thomas, he had lived out the myth we had
made of him. It was some years later that he
married his secretary—after having had such a
disastrous first marriage—and said that he
could hardly believe such happiness would ever
be due him, at the very point when he had given
up all hope.

In my last year, the spring seemed endless,
with no classes to attend and sexual tension in
the air. Jean Valentine and I had already met
before I danced with her at a Lowell House
dance. The first time I was cruel, or so it now
seems, but really I was simply showing off to a

girl who was a freshman and who must have seen me spinning like a top, eager to displease.

Our encounter was at Jim Cronin's. Just off Harvard Square, Cronin's bar and restaurant was row after row of booths, no college paraphernalia, except an oar or two over the bar at which the Cambridge locals—old timers —sat. I came in each night about eleven to case the scene, a social call here and there, drop into a conversation between two graduate students who seemed in 1952 always to be talking about Wordsworth or Wallace Stevens or George Eliot. Girls seldom came alone then, but that night I was looking for Jean because I had her short story in hand, scrawled with marginalia like "won't do," "no," "please," "unclear." I hardly knew her—my friend Barrie Cooke, an English painter who lived in Lowell House and liked my fiction because it sounded like D.H. Lawrence, knew her, and it was supposed to be a kindness for a senior like me to bother with a freshman's short story.

But what did I know of kindness? I had dismissed my own first effort, a short story that was a mishmash of Joyce, Dos Passos and Hemingway, which had occasioned a dreadful review in the *Harvard Crimson*. Now I swaggered about as bits of my first novel appeared in the *Advocate*; Daniel Ellsberg had given me a won-

derful review in the *Crimson,* and praise for
*Advocate* writers was so rare in the college
newspaper that I have always remained grateful
for this singular bit of flattery. Archibald
MacLeish, who taught the advanced writing
seminar, also liked my work. MacLeish's seminar was remarkable for the number of gifted
writers who were admitted—among them in
my years were Harold Brodkey, Ted Hoagland
and Jerry Goodman (who later wrote about
economics under the pseudonym "Adam
Smith"); but more important, MacLeish provided a certain tone—treat the novice writer's
work with respect and don't allow any criticism
to be willfully cruel, in short, no smart-ass re-
marks. For two hours a week we met in his
study at Widener Library, and for a time were
allowed to believe we were serious writers.
Now I was meeting another writer, Jean Valentine, who was later to become a distinguished
poet, whose voice at that time was so delicate it
seemed a leaf could break it, sitting alone in the
booth, waiting for me to tell her what I thought
of the story she had written.

I think now I was callous because I believed it was professional to act so. (A year or
so later I came upon a poem of hers in the *Advocate.* The language just swung along, but how
could I have known?) She sat across from me,

twisting her curly hair in her fingers, hardly
speaking, as I went on, the slayer of unneces-
sary adjectives.

We did not see each other again until that
spring, improbably at a dance. She was with a
classmate, Barrie Cooke again, and I hung
about the dining hall at Lowell House where a
swing band was playing. She danced with me
and then only with me, and for a while Barrie
scowled, then he pulled me roughly aside—I
was stealing his girl even if she wasn't his girl
—"Is this the real thing, Chace?" Absurd question—one evening dancing with a girl I had ver-
bally abused. Carelessly I answered, "Yes."

And I was right. It was the real thing. I was
falling in love.

*"Nel mezzo del cammin di nostra vita—"*
The text of *The Divine Comedy* lay open in
the sunlight. Jean was leaning close to me on
the sofa, small, thin shoulders, her head bent
over the text, for she knew no Italian, and I had
asked her up to my room to translate for her. I
reached for a breast.

"Go on reading."

*"Ahi, quanto a dir qual era e cosa dura /
esta selva selvaggia e aspra e forte—"*

"No."

*"Tant'e amara che poco e piu morte—"*

"You were going to translate."

" 'I cannot rightly say how I entered it, I was so full of sleep when I left the true way—' "

"Get off of me."

"But—*Ma*."

Was I actually chasing her around the room?

The book fell into the fireplace.

"Stop tackling me!"

Even now I believe it was a simple misunderstanding that ended our romance. It was certainly not the tussling during the afternoons, even less the passionate kisses on the steps of Cabot Hall after the chaste walks through the Common and up Concord Avenue to Linnaean Street. I asked Jean to go to the senior dance, and she, in turn, asked me to go with her to the Vineyard where her Boston-rich family had a summer place. Then she went away, and I expected to hear from her. But as the days passed, I became more and more hesitant to call her, angry that I should have heard nothing. That is how it ended. Nothing was said. No one called. I sulked. Maybe she grew afraid of my impulsive behavior—or distrusted her own rash decision. She might not have heard my doubtless mumbled invitation to the dance.

Jean must have seemed my salvation, the promise of manhood to a sexually insecure boy.

But there was more. She held fierce values. She
sought absolute certainty, absolute love.

I saw her again on a train in England, perhaps a year later when I was visiting Barrie
Cooke, who was living in Ireland and starting
to become famous as a painter, and walked
away from her. The slights I imagined she in-
flicted on me would have shattered any man's
self-confidence. But they doubtless were imagined. I ran into her in Harvard Yard while I was
in the army. I made a rude response to her
sweet invitation to ring her up. The third time,
years later, I learned she was rooming with a
mutual friend in New York. I was back from the
army, and I had had a love affair by then—
which I had carelessly thrown away—and
asked her to meet me at the bar of the Plaza
Hotel. It was late May, and Central Park was
blossoming through the windows. We walked
along the cobblestones on Fifth Avenue, and
she was who I wanted—and I married her.

When I left Harvard, I also left Cambridge.
Rawness was missing there. Already I had shed
a spontaneity that I believed naive, but I was
even more fearful of taking risks and seemingly
unable to go it alone. In my junior year I grew
close to Walter Kaiser. He had an unbridled
passion for paintings and would lead me
through the museums of Boston as though we

were on a quest for some supreme principle. He
wrote of Paul Cézanne—the rigor of Cézanne's
landscapes filled him with a wicked joy he believed I shared. And perhaps I did. (I remember
the first work of art I saw that was not a photograph—hands entwined, sculpted by Rodin, in
a glass case in Providence, Rhode Island, where
I had gone on a bus from Fall River on an idle
afternoon.) I have never looked at paintings
with the same ardor as I did when Walter was
guiding me through the Gardner Museum. Walter—after a summer in Europe tutoring the son
of a very rich and distinguished family—became worldly, as though he had finally figured
out what that really meant. I envied him. I was
also determined to emulate him.

In time, I too went to Paris, on a fellowship
to study Baudelaire and Delacroix, while the
war in northeast Asia receded. I had joined
the reserves because I wanted to postpone the
draft, and by going to Paris I thought I could
put politics out of sight altogether. The sadness
of the war came to me only in letters from the
boys from Fall River who were now in Korea—
Jim Kay, one of the old Partisans who had spent
a year at Harvard painting bowls of highly col-
ored flowers and another designing sets for the
Hasty Pudding Club show, and Raymond Medeiros, the most committed aesthete I have ever
known, who had read more than I had, who

wrote better stories and poems, and who enlisted in the army to escape finally from Fall
River. Raymond wrote:

"America, America: I feel as if I have lost it
as a home. Perhaps I have only forgotten it a
little. Quotas, fences, barbed wire. 'Korea picture not too dark.' Tucked away in a corner:
Washington, January 11 (AP)—'Announced
American casualties in Korea now total 42,713,
an increase of 2,537 over a week ago. The total
includes 6,246 killed in action, 29,306
wounded, 7,160 missing.'

"Getting off the streets of Pusan has been a
wonderful thing. There is no poverty, no misery
in the mountains. Leaving behind the shacks
and their shops, one begins to see why this was
called the Land of the Morning Calm."

Paris, May 1954—I could not have been
more mistaken about my escape from politics.
That month Dien Bien Phu fell. It was the last
set-piece battle of the French Army in Indochina. Surrounded by Vietnamese soldiers from
the hills, foolishly isolated in a valley with only
air support to lift their casualties out, the
French troops bravely fought on. The siege
lasted two months and when the doomed army
surrendered, it meant the end of French colo-
nial rule in Asia. Along the Boulevard Saint-
Michel the tides of students swept around the

kiosks. Yet there were no real scuffles, no cries of disbelief. It was not like an assassination, but rather like the needless death of a friend, all wrong. Throughout the long spring we had read of Colonel de Castries, the hero of the besieged redoubt, whose defeat seemed to underline the very absurdity of the struggle. For the Americans who were drawn, often by accident, into the student riots and protests, the siege seemed to connect us to a larger scheme of suffering and judgments than we had ever known. It was not, after all, an American war.

The opposition between art and politics that had seemed inherent at Harvard was being resolved in Paris by how one lived. Yeats had understood it and had come out on the other side, the side we had always understood in Cambridge. He had quoted Thomas Mann: "In our time the destiny of man presents its meaning in political terms," and then went on to counter it: "How can I, that girl standing there / My attention fix / On Roman or on Russian / Or on Spanish politics?" It was a question of a moment in time. If Yeats was finally right, Mann had nonetheless understood the necessity of political commitment at decisive moments in history, and that time, for me, was Paris in 1954.

When I first arrived in the fall of 1953, Paris was sunlit. Even a week before Christmas it was like Indian summer. Samuel Beckett's

*Waiting for Godot* was playing in the small
cramped Theatre de Babylone. Camus and
Sartre railed at each other over the relevance of
Marxism. Gérard Philipe played Don Juan.
Jean-Louis Barrault staged *Phèdre,* with trav-
ertine baroque corridors that drew the tragic
heroine forward, out of the darkness, her head
aching, with ornaments that weighed upon her,
hating the daylight.

My college roommate, Michael Peirce, and
I had not, of course, come to Paris for the politics. We lived in a room in a hotel at 31, rue de
la Harpe, overlooking the courtyard of the
Church of Saint Severin. Our toilet was on the
landing below, and for a shower we walked up
the rue Monsieur le Prince to the Bains Racine.
Michael, who was later to make his living as a
commercial photographer, went off to the out-
lying quarters with light meters hanging from
his neck. Later we bought a British Austin and
drove through the Alps with one of my friends
from junior high school, Jack Sherman, who
was braving the inhospitable winters of Edinburgh studying psychology. Michael took a
photograph of me through sunglasses over the
camera's lens against a mountaintop. In warmer
weather Michael, Jack and I ran with the bulls
in Pamplona and spent time in a brothel in Sal-
amanca. Michael even cut his hair short and

bought his first custom-made suit from an anarchist tailor in Barcelona.

I had come to Paris to look at Delacroix's paintings, read Baudelaire's art criticism and write a novel. My parents were shadowy figures now. I dimly knew that my father's health was failing, though he would live for another ten years. The week before I left the United States, my mother, my father and I had gone to a restaurant at Sakonnet Point. It was a sunny day and only a few cirrus clouds could be seen over Newport. They tried to reassure me that I could always come home if things didn't work out. They also knew that I would probably never live in Fall River again. I remember seeing my father walk over to the juke box at the far end of the dining room. No one else was in the restaurant. He dropped a nickel in to play the Beer Barrel Polka, and as he came back to my mother and me it seemed that the clothes he was wearing hung on him; the jauntiness I associated with his walk and smile had gone away, probably because earning any money was now harder than ever, and I was going too far away to help, and Hollister was out of touch living in Lima, Peru, running a textile mill. The rollicking music was all wrong and suddenly sad. Of course we wrote letters back and forth, with no disturbing news either of us wished to

convey, and from time to time my mother would
send over my favorite dessert, baked meringue
marguerites dropped on a saltine and packed in
a Uneeda biscuit box. They arrived in Paris in
broken pieces that I greedily devoured at my
desk, as I now found myself involved in writing
an opera libretto for a French musician who
composed in the late manner of Stravinsky.

But 1953 was also the high days of the cold
war. It had seemed in the nature of things that
I should have been approached rather mysteri-
ously in the spring of my senior year, after I
had won the fellowship, by a man who extended
a Delphic invitation to see him in New York
about working for the American government in
Paris. It would add to my fellowship money
and, apolitical as I was, I was agreeable to the
idea, without quite knowing what I was supposed to do.

When my meeting in New York was not
followed up, I knew my life as a spy was not
meant to be. I was wrong. It must have been
just before Christmas that I received a call from
another contact who reminded me of my encounter with the government official in New
York. Would I meet him for a *café filtre* at the
Café Cluny? I would and I did. What they (from
whatever branch of the intelligence service *they*
came) wanted from me were reports on the political views of French students. These were to

be presented in lengthy essays I was to hand in, with of course suitable references to the political cal state of France and the activities of the left (whoever and whatever that was).

I accepted. I would become their man on the left bank. And so I became a voyeur of politics. There were meetings, cells of militants who militated against everything—the war in Indochina . . . German rearmament . . . the Socialists . . . the Communists . . . and, naturally, the government. "There is little to choose between the Americans who will soon be in Saigon and the Communists in Hanoi," I was told. Then what were they militating for? "Once you stop struggling against evil, you might as well stop existing as a man." The point was, I was told, that a war six thousand miles from Paris threatened us all, and no one could avoid the consequences of it.

Shabbily dressed men and women seldom filled half the seats in a small room, the dregs of the *Rassemblement du Peuple Français,* the right-wing populist party General de Gaulle had now disavowed. A few years before they would have filled the stadium of the Vel d'Hiver. *They* weren't militants; they were, instead, a remnant, those who had been betrayed —betrayed by a government that was losing a war and debasing the currency—and deserted by de Gaulle himself, who was finally to betray

them four years later in Algiers when he
showed he understood that Algeria must be
free.

My knowledge of French politics grew as I
forced myself to read the small type of the un-
readable newspaper, *Le Monde*. My reports,
sketchy at first, became more authoritative. I
was especially praised by my contact for my
prediction—which came true in less than three
months—that Pierre Mendès-France, an obscure politician to Americans, would become
prime minister with a mandate to settle the war
in Indochina. This I learned after reading a particularly prescient article in the *Partisan Review* at the American Library on the Boulevard
Saint-Germain.

But my greatest achievement turned out to
be my contention that the European Defense
Community—a device designed to weld the
French armed forces to the German and other
West European armies—would never come into
being. Although the French foreign minister du-
tifully informed his American counterpart that
the defense community would be voted on fa-
vorably, I couldn't find anyone who favored it.
Not the concierge. Not the French students I
polled in my bistro on the rue de la Harpe. Now
if the British had been willing to join in, it
would have been a different matter. The British, however, clung to the remnants of empire

and their doomed attachment to the Americans
—Greeks to our Romans, as they foolishly believed. And the French were too fearful of being
locked into a military organization with the
Germans. In the National Assembly the European Defense Community failed. My reputation
soared. (Did no American experts read *Le
Monde,* I wondered. Though one could hardly
blame them. *I* was their reader.)

Characteristically, life imitated art. My
contact, an old Harvardian garbed in chino
pants and horn-rimmed glasses, insisted that
my reports be handed over in such a way as to
conceal our acquaintance from the meddling
French. I was to go to the Café Viel on the rue
Royale, pretend to be reading the *Herald Tri-
bune* by punching a hole through the paper so I
could catch sight of him as he entered the café
and then place my incriminating document
under a folded copy of the *Trib.* Another bright
idea was to meet at the bar of Air France at the
Gare d'Orsay, which seemed to me to be the
very epicenter of espionage.

The problem, I was told, was that the
French were probably on to us—there were
counterspies everywhere—and had undoubt-
edly tapped my contact's phone. Were our allies
to arrest me, my compatriots would have to
deny any knowledge of my activities. Moreover,
I soon found out that the French *were* on to me:

the concierge told me she had been called down
to the commissariat to be questioned about me.
Later, mail I received seemed to have been
steamed open. Surveillance, a French specialty
since the days of Louis IX, was the order of the
day. The game, as I was told, was did the
French know that we knew that the French
knew?—a question that could be repeated end-
lessly.

The end came when I was to return home
on the *Ile de France*. So cogent were my reports
that I was being offered a new post—as a full-
time agent—in Florence. I might have accepted
had my final meeting not hinted at the dangers
ahead. I had been told to thumb a ride into the
Bois de Boulogne, a singularly foolish idea, it
seemed to me, as I stood in the late afternoon
sun on the avenue Foch. My contact spun
around the bend in his Morris Minor and I
climbed in. My report—a summing-up of
French follies under the Fourth Republic, cou-
pled with a guarded hope that Charles de
Gaulle would emerge from his solitude to restore the republic to greatness—lay on the seat
between us. Suddenly, a French police car bore
down on us, and the game was surely up. We
were forced to the side of the road. The gen-
darme was polite but firm. We were speeding.
The dossier on the seat lay unread.

I never saw my contact again. I became, moreover, a confirmed Gaullist, the more so when I spent the next two years on detached service from the U.S. Army to the French Army not far from the General's brooding retreat in Lorraine.

Things might have turned out differently. Leaving Paris, I went to London for two weeks to visit Barrie Cooke. He had chosen to live in Ireland where he could shoot and trout-fish and live on nothing at all, and he proposed a hiking expedition along the river Test in Hampshire, one of the great trout-fishing streams in England. Michael was to put my bags on the *Ile de France* at Le Havre, and I would board at Southampton.

By the time I hooked up with Barrie for our walking trip, I was involved with a girl I had met in London in a flat I was sharing with her and two other women I had known fleetingly. Scottish, alien in London, Marian was excessively shy: she would bite her lower lip in embarrassment if she thought she was asking too much: another drink at the pub or more time walking in Saint James's Park. What drew me to her was her quick and loving response to a phrase of music or to the unfashionably painterly canvases of Fragonard that I especially liked. Like Jean Valentine, she seemed, in her soft-spoken way, to be particularly strict in her tastes.

But in ten days I was sailing to America to go into the army, and I couldn't permit myself to fall in love as I was doing, as I believed she was doing, as we lingered in the Tate Gallery or held hands in movie theaters. Nothing was said. My leaving made it impossible for me to say anything about my feelings for her and she was doubtless bewildered by what was happening.

I decided on a dramatic gesture. Marian planned to see me off at the boat train at Victoria Station. I would ask her to board the train with me and on the journey to Southampton tell her that I had fallen in love. If she felt the same way, I would tell Michael I was not going to America and phone my contact in Paris to tell him I accepted the job as a secret agent in Florence.

But on the morning I was to leave—since nothing had been said—the other two roommates decided to go with us to the station. I was stunned. Helpless and grieving, I stood next to Marian. The next moment I was watching the three girls from the window of the coach, waving me goodbye. Muted passion indeed. I was thoroughly undone.

Some time later I heard that Marian was engaged to an English doctor. On leave from the army I visited London and in a generous mood contacted Marian and her beloved. She was leaving for Scotland and we were to meet in King's Cross Station. But taxis were hard to find, and by the time I got there Marian was standing on the steps of the coach as the train moved slowly out of the station toward Edinburgh. I waved at her from the platform and then went off with her doctor friend to drink into the night. It didn't take too much to tell him that I had fallen in love with Marian a year or so earlier but had been unable to tell her so, what with my cowardice, my virtual certainty of her rejection. "But didn't you know," he said, "she was in love with you."

My choosing to be drafted into the U.S. Army finally broke me from the dependency I had always sought. As I marched across the parade ground of Fort Dix, I felt exhilarated at being so cut off. My sensations seemed more acute—watching the streaky dawn in the icy darkness or listening for the quick crack of a rifle bullet against the distant sand pits. I became friendly with a group of young kids from Brooklyn who flattered me by asking me to go with them on a weekend pass to hijack a truck loaded with whiskey. It was cool to be asked, and it was cool to refuse. The atmosphere during basic was oddly tolerant. No one was mocked—neither the effeminate boy nor the intellectual who read Yeats nor the comic-book junkie—so disoriented were we all, stunned by the arbitrary and the absurd.

After the second eight weeks of basic training, we sat in a classroom at Fort Dix and waited to see what the assignment would be. No one would have chosen the Far Eastern Command, and when the names were called for Korea, there was silence. Later, the lucky ones who, like myself, were being sent to Europe, avoided those who had lost in the lottery. One other recruit, André Kaufman, and I were going to Europe, and with any luck, brandishing our assignments as French interpreters, would find the good life in France. *Fröhlich wie Gott im Frankreich,* he said: Happy as God in France.

André Kaufman, pale, rheumy-eyed cynic, his face white as a clown's, with powder slapped on to disguise his unshaven cheeks, French enough, after the years in Hollywood with his father, to hang a Lucky Strike from his lips like a Gauloise, André and I pulled into the Gare d'Austerlitz at the crack of dawn. Cocky in our uniforms we split, each to discover his own memory of what it had been like in Paris only six months earlier, before the army. I returned to the rue de la Harpe to find the hotel in the last stages of disintegration, the concierge talking too much about the *servitudes et gran-*

*deurs militaires* of the French Army in Algeria, with more stress on the servitude than the grandeur.

Verdun the next morning seemed an enormous distance from Paris, though it was only four hours by Volkswagen. But my assignment as liaison to the French Army gave me more freedom of action than working in an office of the U.S. Army in Europe. I was billeted at the Caserne Maginot, a great gray stone barracks built in the first years of the Third Republic, and here I was to live with the Americans while spending days in a small office near the river Meuse with my French counterparts. It was said that Verdun was sympathetic to soldiers, for it had been a garrison since the ninth century. The town itself was constructed around the Citadel, a massive stone armory that housed the French headquarters of the engineers as well as serving as the centerpiece for a motorcycle track. My own situation lent itself to a peculiar freedom: neither responsible to my American commanding officer in the Caserne nor under the direct authority of the French, I was let loose to travel about the countryside seeking land that was to be acquired by the U.S. Army, Advanced Section, Communications Zone, France.

The war inhabited this place. *Ici fut Fleury* —a small headstone by the side of the road

marked where a village had once existed. Farther on lay the Trench of Bayonets, a fragment
of a trench where the men standing in it, their
rifles fixed, had been buried alive, their guns
still held in skeletal fingers, kept as a memorial
to the war dead. Driving the jeep along the road
between the neatly cultivated fields, I tried to
imagine my Uncle Gardner, who had himself
fought not far from Verdun (and whose failings
were always put down to having been gassed in
the war). Only in the morning in winter, when
the mists hung over the fields and the barbed
wire was no longer tangled in weeds and vines,
could I drive these roads and imagine myself a
soldier in the early years of the great European
civil war. But these fantasies were necessarily
short-lived: a large motor pool and complex
called Chicago marked the entrance to Verdun
like a used car lot.

To give the gloominess its due, the French
had constructed at Fort Douaumont the most
fitting monument to the useless slaughter.
There, near the site of the fort, opposite the grid
of white crosses, the *ossuaire* of Douaumont
rose in absolute phallic splendor above a marble tomb. Imagine a railway station and inside
the light a pale amber and the walls inscribed
with the names of the dead; along the walls, like
coffins, squares of marble were also inscribed
to commemorate the fallen: Gift of the City of

Philadelphia, or some such. A trip to this empty
mortuary would hardly seem worth it: it's
mostly German tourists anyway who come. But
walk behind the great tomb and you can see
along the bottom a kind of cellar window
painted over black. There, stooping low to
glance inside where the paint has been
scratched away, you can see why the monument
is known as a bonery. The massive structure is
literally built upon the fragments of human
bones, bits of skeleton not arranged as in some
orderly Capuchin catacomb, all dressed to kill,
but the true boneyard of this century—scat-
tered, broken skulls and ribs and thighs inter-
mingled with shrapnel to make a foundation for
the barren monument above.

Verdun, then, where a million men on both
sides died, wastage as never before, its defo-
liated land only barely covered over with grass,
lay in the path of the next invader. The old forts
still stood, and who could say if they were ever
to be used again? The American troops at Headquarters, ADSEC, were there to keep the lines
open to our army in Germany, and every few
months there was an alert when we prepared
for war. Major Hancock, standing before us, his
arms outstretched, bellowed in the early morning formation: "I can hold off the Russian bear
when it comes over the hill, with just you men."
But the Russians were not about to come. The

European civil war was over. Stalin was dead.
The continent had been divided between the
two great powers—and neither America nor
Russia would break the peace, at least not here
in Europe where the lines had been drawn and
the rules of the cold war were respected.

On days of Alert I rejoined the American
Army, abandoning my French comrades to the
easier duty of tending U.S. Army real estate.
(There were few French soldiers about in any
case, for almost all the young officers were in
Algeria with the conscripts; older comman-
dants and civilian ex-colonials manned the Citadel now.) Packed into trucks, the rifles rising
hard between our thighs, desk jockeys untimely
ripped from our offices, we were sullen recruits
for the Major's battle plan. Ronald Steel, the
general's interpreter and a friend of mine ever
since I discovered him in the dining hall reading a copy of a French newspaper, sat near me
in his dirty fatigues leafing through a battered
copy of *Le Monde*. I muttered something about
General de Gaulle coming back into power and
getting France out of Algeria.

"Yeah? What about Indochina? What about
getting us out of Vietnam?" Ron posed the question sleepily, then smiled and went back to
reading the news. He waved at me as I dropped
off the tailgate.

The hill I was to guard held no terrors. In

the stillness I was the child in the grass looking
for the spy to emerge into the sunlight, or the
plane spotter on the Flatiron Building scanning
the sky for a silhouette other than a crow. On
another hill a rusty gun emplacement poked
out. The white sun rose higher. But something
was amiss.

I don't know how long it must have been
before I reacted to a woman's crying. In fact, it
wasn't really a cry but more like a moan, and I
began tracking the sound out of curiosity. When
I finally came on her, she was huddled by the
road in a ball, and sobbing. Four or five soldiers
stood around while the sergeant interrogated
her.

The noncom bent close to this American
bride, hardly out of high school, and held her
by the shoulders. "Tell me, ma'am." And the
story came out: her husband, a recently arrived
G.I., was lost in the underground corridors of
an old fort. Exhausted after her search, fearful
that she had done something wrong, she had
hidden by the side of the road. "I was afraid,
sir. We knew we broke the rules."

The search party justified the alert. Command posts were set up. Troops were moved
and mobilized, the eastern hills abandoned to
the Russians. Even the lawyers from the Judge
Advocate's office materialized in fatigues. By
noon, field kitchens had been set up behind the

abandoned fort, and the company commander was organizing the first search group.

No one seemed to have a plan of the fort's interior, so we proceeded by flashlight; at the first opportunity an auxiliary power station was to be set up. Our logistics were excellent, though the wife was no help. Hysterical at the end, she left us as we explored the darkness under the direction of the Major's bullhorn. Stringing out a rope to guide us back, or to help us should we fall, we paused every twenty feet, called out the soldier's name, waited, stumbled, cursed, and stepped forward again. It was absurd that he should have gone so far, against all odds, into such a labyrinth. But I didn't know what he was like. No one I knew knew him.

It took about three hours to find him. Like the boy who had finally penetrated my basement redoubt in Fall River and fallen into the cistern, the soldier had tumbled down a shaft. But in this case, he was dead.

A few days later the fort where the soldier fell became yet another landmark at Verdun: until the American army left ten years later, it was especially useful as a warning to new troops.

Verdun, then, was my war, a phony war as it turned out with our troops prepared to fight an enemy that had no intention of attacking the

West. We were in fixed positions in 1954, guarding the presumed invasion route over the Rhine River as my father's and my brother's generations had. For the next four decades American soldiers remained in Europe, even though we were expelled from France by General de Gaulle in 1966. But we fought the cold war in every part of the globe, with troops in Korea and Vietnam, sailors in the Persian Gulf and the South China Sea, marines in Lebanon, and surrogate soldiers—the so-called contras—in Central America. I finally came closest to actual combat in Central America in the 1980s, surely the last frontier of the cold war, and probably its closing battle.

I was on assignment at the time, visiting the town of Ocotal in northern Nicaragua. Along with Chris Dickey, a correspondent from the *Washington Post,* and Mark Uhlig, a young editor from *Foreign Affairs,* I was looking for the rebel guerrillas who were coming across the Honduran border to harass the Sandinista militiamen. We wanted to see the actual state of siege that prevailed along the Coco River.

The bridge over the river had been shattered. But the water seemed fordable. So we asked some Nicaraguan soldiers in a jeep to tow our Toyota sedan through the water. In high spirits, at last we found ourselves at the end of the day in a rally in the main square. Young

men were being exhorted to drive out the coun-
terrevolutionaries. Then they were given rifles
and put onto trucks as darkness came. They
were being sent across the river to reconnoiter
in the hills and forestall any invaders who
might try to seize the town. In the courtyards,
air raid shelters were being dug for those too
young and too old to fight. Ocotal was at war.
That night we were the only guests in the Hotel
de la Frontiera, which sat on the riverbank.
When total darkness came and the lights were
put out, the gunfire came—mortars and 50-cal-
iber machine guns, bullets so close at times it
seemed the hotel itself was under siege. We
whispered in the darkness or tried to sleep
under mattresses or simply waited for the
dawn.

High in the hills, the gunfire grew finally
softer and softer. It was, after all, a war made
by partisans, as almost all wars now seem to
be.

# Looking
# for Billie Holiday

I caught up with Billie Holiday in her middle period, sometime before V-J day in 1945, when she came to Fall River, billed, improbably, with Gene Krupa's band. I went to see her at the old Casino boxing arena. She was singing at that time with what Elizabeth Hardwick has called "the miracle of pure style." Earlier on, her music, effortless, contained only hints of darkness, though the catch in her voice when she held the notes longer and longer before her final coda should have told us that she knew something more than how the voice could become an instrument for jazz. In her last period she used phrasing that bent jazz out of shape—there has never been anything like it before, and it is hard to imagine anything so dominating ever again.

I had heard her voice from before the war,

on the one record Hollister owned of her, "Easy
Living." He often played it and danced to it
when his girl friend, Pat Walsh, came by, and
so along with Pat's laughter and sighs were the
sounds of Billie Holiday, and I must have imagined the darker side of love. When I came
across a new rendition of "Easy Living" four
years later, her voice had thickened, the notes
were broken, and the exaggerated line of the
lyric expressed far more explicitly those hints
of irony that had been present earlier when
Hollister and Pat closeted themselves apart on
the second floor.

It was Pat I thought I had lost when Hollister, in the first violent year of his homecoming
after the war, once again demanded that she
marry him. But again she refused him. Then,
after her escape from Hollister, she married my
cousin Gardner. Theirs grew to be a large family, but by then Hollister had gone off to South
America and Pat and young Gardner lived near
my father and mother, like son and daughter,
caring for them in the long years after their first
illnesses. Pat came hardly to resemble the
woman I remembered from before the war. It
was not so much her physical appearance, for,
like my mother's, it changed slowly—her skin
was drawn tightly over her cheekbones and
chin—but rather it was her connection to Hollister, to Billie Holiday's song, that became re-

mote, unrecognizable. She was becoming almost too good for this world.

My own rediscovery of Billie Holiday in the late 1940s was a further opening to the longings I felt for a world elsewhere. There was no jazz in Fall River, no music at all, really, unless you happened upon it because someone played the violin or the piano. There was the Philharmonic on CBS on Sunday afternoons and Texaco's Metropolitan Opera on Saturdays—but that pretty much passed me by. So I was left with jazz, a taste that was abetted by two friends, one an outsider from the Midwest whose family had recently come east, and the other, a pale boy with bad teeth, a couple of years older than I, an outsider in his manner of somehow looking askance at his environment. He worked in a record store and became a part-time disc jockey for the local radio station. He was already listening to bop, while I still collected Dixieland and swing, Chicago and Kansas City, but always Billie Holiday. I even made a trip to New York, some six hours away, to visit a record store I had read of: all I did was ride the bus and walk up Sixth Avenue to 46th Street to a storefront filled with new and second-hand Okeh, Bluebird and Vocalion records, buy a few Billie Holidays, and return home. New York City hardly existed for me.

I was just fourteen when I heard her at the

Fall River Casino. Her set began at midnight, and I had to get permission from my parents to stay out that late. She came on stage wearing a gardenia in her hair, just as the record albums showed her, and when she sang her body was still, except for the slight movement of the head, fingers snapping together in time with the beat. The black audience—almost all from Providence or New Bedford—packed the boxing arena and fell absolutely silent as she began to sing.

I saw her three more times. As an undergraduate, I heard her sing unevenly at the Latin Quarter and bought her a drink at the bar. Too tangled up to speak, I got nothing back from her. A shrug perhaps, a muttered thank you. Then, a year or so before her death in the late 1950s, she sang triumphantly at Carnegie Hall, and I brought my wife along to hear her. (Because of her conviction for drug use, she was not permitted to sing in clubs.) Then I went to an outdoor concert in Central Park, when her performance broke down and those listening seemed scarcely aware of whom they were listening to. Finally, I went to her funeral at the Roman Catholic Church behind Columbus Circle. My oldest daughter was a baby at the time, and the old 78 rpm records had been given away by mistake to the Salvation Army by my father and were being replaced by long-playing discs. Jazz was starting to go out of favor, even in New York.

Jazz seemed so alluring it became almost a secret vice for me. My friendship with Raymond Medeiros seemed equally illicit. With the most improbable of names, Raymond was a Portuguese boy with English grandparents. He, too, was demonic under his soft-spoken manner. Quite simply, when I met him as a sophomore in high school, he had read more books than anyone I had ever encountered. He would sit smoking Camel cigarettes for hours as he alternately praised me for loving Hawthorne and excoriated me for my indifference to politics, to justice, and finally to the revolution.

Nonetheless, because of Raymond I read Marx and Engels. Raymond brought me to a Friendly Henry Wallace rally in New Bedford during the 1948 campaign. "What you have to understand, Jimmy, is that William James— who knew what he was talking about—said that so far war's been the only force that can discipline a whole community, and until an equivalent discipline is organized, war must have its way. Well, it's up to us to organize a different discipline."

Having left the Partisans to history, I sought out Raymond, who managed to combine his commitment to Marx with an attraction to

Baudelaire. I, in turn, spent my days with Raymond in a coffee shop listening to him, learning from him, envying him his absolute commitment to literature, to radical politics, to the dark world that was so seductive and so terrifying. But in the evenings I left him for the endless card games with girls I barely knew, or hours in a car across the river with Barbara or Ann or whomever, stumbling home at dawn breathless and weary, while Raymond implied by his silence that he saw only wastage in those white nights.

The late 1940s were the merest beginning of America's postwar hunt for Reds. I knew we were considered subversives during the 1948 Wallace campaign, that going to Progressive Party rallies was something out of line, not just breaking the rules as I did when I drank gin with other friends late on a summer evening, followed by a nude swim in the river. Raymond knew differently; he saw, as he put it then, "the spectacle of mankind in chains and deprivation in a world of freedom and plenty."

A few months after Truman was elected, Raymond disappeared. He must have gone during Christmas vacation, when I was caught up with preparing for the formal dance and deciding how to break up with my girl friend. At the time, Raymond had stopped talking politics and, so I thought, had gone back to literature, when he was not arguing Catholic doctrine with a would-be Jesuit down from Holy Cross.

After the holidays, having behaved badly to my girl friend at the Christmas dance when I let her go home with the aspiring Jesuit, I expected to resume my dialogue with Raymond. But Raymond had gone. I was bewildered. Of course, he had not confided in me because I had been so self-absorbed, so indifferent to him during those excessively social interludes. But others expected me to know where he had gone —and why. Weeks passed. I heard nothing and knew nothing. Then I was called to the Principal's office for an interrogation.

Old Mr. Carroll was a remote figure presiding over about two thousand students at Durfee High School. The curriculum was much as it had been for fifty years, the best teachers at least that old, and the only significant change the spectacular victories of the basketball team, which had won the state and New England championships. Mr. Carroll asked me in an awkward, gruff tone of voice, as though he were puzzled and embarrassed that I should be there at all and he an inquisitor, whether Raymond was a Communist. I was his closest friend, he was told, and it now appeared that Raymond had been found in Boston, apprehended by the police, and would soon be on his way back to his family and school. I don't know if I denied the accusation or simply dodged the questions by evasions. But I remember saying that I knew nothing of where he had been or why, insisting rather too hotly for Mr. Carroll's taste, that I was his friend, whatever happened.

Raymond came back. Nothing was said or done officially. Mr. Carroll was doubtless relieved at the silence that attended his return. Although the Berlin blockade was being broken, in Fall River the talk was about jobs, as the last textile mills closed. Raymond's father was likely to be unemployed. Raymond told me something of what had happened, but only in fragments. How he had gone to Boston and found comfort and brotherhood with members of a Communist cell, of "hootenannies" where they sang songs of solidarity. I seem to recall his telling me of being held closely by a loved one in the night, and then the discovery of him as a missing person by the police. He was hurt by the cop who burned a cigarette into his nipple because he might be a Communist, but he spoke of all this as though it had happened in a foreign country a long time ago.

It was, I learned many years later, his second attempt to escape. His first was when he was twelve and came upon a tramp who was living in the woods near the reservoir. He seemed to Raymond a free spirit, and yet perhaps he was a fugitive. They became friends. It was spring, the late spring of Massachusetts, when branches hardly show any buds before the end of April—except for the forsythia that decorated the tramp's campsite along the pond. As Raymond put it when he was trying to explain it to me: "Everyone's heart's desire is really this: Come, travel with me. Shall we stick by each other as long as we live? Well, few get their heart's desire."

The vagabond must have known he'd got more than he bargained for when he befriended Raymond. He apparently agreed to take Raymond with him, and they set their escape for early one morning before the spring became summer and the highway hot. I wonder now if the tramp planned what transpired—it would have been easy enough to have decamped under cover of night. In any event, a car soon stopped for the hitchhikers. It was a two-door coupe, and Raymond got in first, in the back. Then the tramp, without a word, slammed the door, motioned the driver to go on without him, and disappeared into the woods. By the time Raymond got the driver to stop and went off in search of the tramp, it was already too late. In revenge, he burned down the lean-to camp by the forsythia.

For Raymond, the consequences of his Boston adventure were long lasting. He missed taking his college boards and the scholarships that might have resulted from them. When I went to Harvard, Raymond stayed behind, bewildered and bursting with intensity, working as a soda jerk in a drugstore. He was writing furiously in those years and described to me in letters his life in Fall River. An encounter with old Mr. Carroll: Inquiring of Raymond's family, he asks about his mother, who had been sick and was reason enough for Raymond to remain at home, "I suppose you help her as much as you can." Raymond answers as he mixes a Fresh Fruit Strawberry Ice Cream soda: "Yes, I feel that there's a lot I have to make up for."

Mr. Carroll: "You mean the way you acted during your last year in high school?"

Raymond: "Yes. At times I feel more guilty than I should."

Mr. Carroll: "Well, everybody has a period of foolishness before they grow up."

Raymond: "Yes, but mine was somewhat more violent than most."

Mr. Carroll: "No. The only thing was that more people knew about it."

So, it turned out, did the army. There was no way Raymond was going to be allowed to stay in Fall River writing poetry and fiction while the Korean War was on and American troops were being pushed back down the peninsula. Thinking of a way to go on with his writing in what promised to be easier circumstances than an infantry unit in the mountains, Raymond enlisted in an army intelligence unit. By the time basic training was over, the discovery of Raymond's schoolboy adventures among the Reds marked him out as someone who would never be permitted to serve in army intelligence. But Raymond was not discharged as an undesirable subversive. Instead, he was simply transferred to an infantry company and sent to Korea, "The Land of the Morning Calm."

His letters started coming—two and three a month—from Korea in 1953. He wrote me of the prostitutes who could never marry because there was a death penalty (beheading) for any who did, whether or not the husband was aware of her previous profession. But most passionately, he wrote me of the landscape: "One felt that these mountains could be called by tender names, could be loved. The soul remembered Eden, for there were melons that should have broken of their own strong sweetness, muscat grapes the size of plums, crickets that sang so loud it must have been with some joy." He may have found himself, as he put it, "alone in a strange country, in poverty of possessions," but there were the mountains and the groves: "No sound but the light wind, a silence so vast that the trickling of a brook or the falling of water off a stone could not even crack the silence as lightning cracks the sky."

Raymond came home from Korea, and by that time I had gone to Europe. For a time he went to Harvard, thanks to the G.I. bill and a man he met from the Harvard Club of Japan who told him to go ahead and apply. But for reasons that were obscure to me—perhaps he was too old for the eighteen-year-olds at play— he left Harvard in his sophomore year and came to New York, where we saw each other again. By that time I was struggling on very little money with my wife and two small children, and Raymond seemed obsessed with Eastern religions. By the 1960s he had left America seemingly forever, gone to Indonesia to follow the religious leader he had found in New York. I have seen him only twice in over twenty years. But he thrives in Indonesia, gray, "wondrously fat," he claims in a letter that comes once a decade. "This place," he writes, "is rich in things of the heart."

It was only to Raymond that I was able to admit how scared I was of the craziness that raged within me but had always been masked at school. Even before I made the conscious effort in fifth grade to adjust to schoolboy life on the playground and at recess, to play hard at

football even though I was too small to do much
good, I had always behaved well in the classroom. Though I had few friends in the lower
grades, I was not particularly sorry for myself.
I gave out valentines on February 14th, asked
Marie Silvia to marry me, and clowned my way
into making new friends, played free-all in the
rocky schoolyard, passed notes, had horse
chestnut fights, built a snow-and-ice fort, collected the papers at the end of class, went to
Sunday school, walked home in the June street
patrol. But then at home I took a knife and tore
through my mother's dresses hanging in the
closet, threatened the neighborhood by turning
on the gas in the cellar nearby, poured potas-
sium in the milk delivered next door, broke into
a police barn, and leaped from couches and
porches until I had to be pinned down.

I decorated a room for myself in the broom
closet of the living room—a stool, a light, a tiny
radio—and there I felt free, as though the
whirling violence that seemed to begin in my
bowels and spiraled upward until I could
hardly breathe were stilled. The family con-
ducted their life beside me and apart from me.
My mother's spinster cousin, Sallie, would
come to visit us once a year, an ugly exotic from
New York who wore elaborate hats and spoke
in a sing-song whine. She once made me climb
into the steeple of what she believed was Paul

Revere's Old North Church—only it was the wrong church, as even I should have known by the dust and decay in the attic. Her life centered around her illnesses, even as she insisted on remaining in New York City in a one-bedroom apartment under, it appeared, the George Washington Bridge. "So many fantastic things have happened," I heard her tell my mother, "yet in a way, nothing. Yes, it's been an obstacle course. But nothing happened really." Sallie was mad, I believed then and believe now, mad in the same way I was. And I could fall in love with craziness. Or at least with those who acted that way.

Was Hollister, too, crazy in some way? Was he even—dare I say it—even linked in some way to my own derangement? In those years before the war when I lay all but naked under a sunlamp and smashed myself against a wall, I can remember his hand on my chest pressing me down in the darkness, I can remember being held in the darkness of our clothes closet and the warm urine dribbling down my leg.

"Hollister was always crazy," my cousin Lois tells me. "It wasn't just after the war." Hollister who, shaking with malaria after the war, grasped my arm so tightly I could not break away. Hollister, who threw me against the glass door of the house and ripped my hand open only a few weeks later. Hollister, who came back a hero with his Bronze Star and his Purple Heart, striking me at the dining room table or pulling me, half-naked, out of the bathroom because I was hiding.

All my own madness seemed to go away when Hollister went away to the war. Now it comes back only in spasms. Most of the time I feel it like a tight wire coiled in my gut, held in place by my commitment to the order of things, arranging bits and pieces of my life against the threatening danger within. After Hollister's return, when he raged against my father for trying to make do with the least possible effort, I became the good son. I behaved the way the world expected me to behave.

Hollister died of a heart attack in his forties. He was still running the textile mill in Peru. I had not seen him for several years, and our last encounter was characteristically painful. Crazy, even. He had come to New York and was staying in a penthouse room at the Sherry Netherland Hotel. I was to meet him for a drink and dinner. He talked about the Communist threat in Peru, and then the leftist threat in the United States. We went across to the Plaza for our late supper and sat next to a table of show-business celebrities, one of whom was a black singer. Suddenly Hollister started complaining loudly to a waiter about being seated next to a

black man. It was absurd. I rushed him from
the restaurant to the cold street. "Why did you
do that?" I asked. "Why did you get mad at a
black man? We never did that at home. What
were you doing? What possessed you?" He
laughed. "I just wanted to see you squirm."

He was buried in Lima, and it was about
ten years later that I finally got there. I meant
to visit his grave, and to this end I sought out
his best friend. He told me that not long before
Hollister died, my brother and he had come
back from a carousing trip along the Altiplano,
the high Andes around Cuzco. He suggested I
take a similar trip, which would also include a
journey to Machu Picchu.

The flight to Cuzco was made in a two-
engine plane. In the cabin we sucked oxygen as
we rose from sea level to the over 11,000-foot-
high city, once the capital of the Inca empire,
with temples and palaces but in 1971 a desolate
city of impoverished Quechua Indians. In the
hours after landing, I lay in a hotel room and
took more oxygen and ate sucrose and waited
for the buzzing in my head to evaporate. Later
I visited the old walls of the city, ruins of the
Inca builders, those architects and planners
whose art was like the Romans', all engineering
and road-building to link an empire that ran
from Ecuador to Chile. The Quechua stared at
us from the roadsides, offering their rough

sweaters for sale. They would stand for hours, half-stoned from constant chewing of the coca leaf to dull their appetites. Their faces were caked with dirt. Here in the Altiplano, the brown barren mountains and the massive stones deadened sound. I remember the silence. One drink of alcohol and the mind goes spinning. And I imagined Hollister spinning as he bought drinks for everyone at the bar in Cuzco, in this barren land where most everyone drinks pale-green doped-up tea.

The next day I boarded the train to the jungle, to Machu Picchu, to that last redoubt of the Incas, their kingdom in ruins, pursued by the conquistadors on their terrifying horses. The train zigzagged down the mountain, and hours later we were riding through the thick leafy foliage, again stared at by Indians. Now rolling through the humid lowlands where we drank and laughed, I kissed a blue-eyed American who had somehow fled the Peace Corps in Bolivia and was heading into the sun on this roller-coaster Tinkertoy train.

Machu Picchu was invisible from the valley. It seemed just another peak. But we were put on buses, and when we reached the mountaintop, there was the city itself, ruined walls and arches and hundreds of steps. Yet there was nothing that could be called a work of art. It was the fact of the city that was so remark-

able, that it should have survived the plunder-
ers for so long, a bowl on an emerald
mountaintop with the clouds below it, a city
that floated. Did Hollister spend the night there
in the small hotel at the entrance to the city?
Did he drink and watch the moon spin?

There was, after all, nothing to see after
you had arrived at your destination. I had come
to an edge of the world, as my brother did, as
far away from Fall River as we could go. But
the steps led nowhere. The stones were huge,
but there was no fortress, and the site itself was
exposed to all kinds of weather. Even as I
climbed aimlessly, the sun grew so hot I felt
faint. I actually needed help to make my way
back to the bus. When we finally reached the
valley again, Machu Picchu had disappeared.

(A year later I might not have survived the
ascent to Cuzco. Like my brother, I had a heart
attack. Once again I had climbed a steep hill on
a fiery hot afternoon, only this time, later that
day, I felt the numbness first in my hands and
then the pain cutting my left arm from my wrist
to my shoulder and then down the center of my
chest, a knife wound that threw me to my bed
for three hours until the pain passed and it
seemed I would live. Back in Lima my brother
must have felt the same pain, the same tingling
in his fingers, and yet when the pain passed he
was dead. And my father, lying on the sofa in

the small pink living room in Fall River as my mother watched him, must have also fallen back on the cushions as the pain in his chest knifed through him. Gaunt at the end, his eyes bulging, he died that night, and then my mother called up my cousin Gardner and asked him to come over because she thought that Holly was dead. The last thing he said was that all he had to leave her was his two sons.)

I returned to Lima the next day and did not bother finding my brother's grave. Instead I drank a lot, and the blue-eyed Peace Corps girl and I decided to visit the erotic museum where the Incas did indeed exhibit artistic inclinations, with household pottery shaped into genitals, a phallus for a spout and vaginas at the openings of serving bowls.

# Fireworks

The Fourth of July in 1944 was the beginning of manhood—eighth grade—and we knew that the war was won. D-Day had already happened. By now my cousin Gardner had been discharged and by the next Fourth, surely my brother Hollister would be with us. There was more family than usual at Aunt Sue and Uncle Dick's for the celebration, and because it *was* the Fourth, Dick made his appearance late in the day in order to set up the fireworks in the garden.

What I remember of that particular Fourth begins with the ride to the country, with me in the rumble seat of the Ford. Staring at the river, at the yellow fields of dandelions, and expecting the long day at Sue's to be mine, I anticipated the taste of chocolates from the sideboard, as I reached up to the silver dish glistening in the

sunlight. From the sunporch the land ran
straight down to the sea, as though its wildness
on that side, the barn tangled in vines, was
planned to complement the narrow entrance-
way of planted flowers and privet.

Sue stood in the doorway as the car came
down the hill. She was serene, took after her
mother who had borne the twelve children, my
father and my aunts and uncles: only six left
then, and Sue childless. That day, besides my
parents and me, there were my Uncle Gardner,
my Aunt Ellen, their two children—my cousins,
young Gardner and Lois; since I was the youngest, I was blessedly ignored.

The house first. I knew the grown-ups
would gather on the sunporch, the cousins in
the adjacent room to play records on the vic. In
the living room there were forty volumes of the
romances of Alexandre Dumas that I could
read, stories of politics in action, a king saved,
a queen exposed by the accidental, the contin-
gent: a lost necklace, a lame horse. Later, after
midday dinner, I would swim; and then dusk
and the first pinwheels. Upstairs the bedrooms
were gabled. I stood at each window gauging
the angle of a sailboat I coveted as it swung at
its mooring. Below the gardens and the fields
and the arbor, beyond the point of the dock the
catboat swung in a slow, winding arc. And Sue
told me she would buy me such a boat next

year. To take it and sail out of the bay beyond the Newport light—there you would feel free, hanging from the windward gunwale, hand on the tiller and the sheet tearing at one's left hand. Islands loomed: beyond the Vineyard lay Nantucket and the Azores, Europe and darkness.

Laughter from below. I squinted into the sunlight, drawing an azimuth with my eye from the railroad bridge to the gong buoy and to the vanishing point beyond the spire of the Mount Hope Bridge. Mount Hope itself was a soft hill: it was there they hunted down King Philip, born Metacomet, chief of the Wampanoags, and killed him in a copse. Before the war I had spent a day with my father searching for King Philip's throne. All the treaties with his father, who had ruled when the settlers first landed, had been broken. It seemed there were no choices left. Betrayed by a Christianized "praying Indian," slain and the war ended, the supremacy of the Wampanoags and the Narragansetts brought down, Philip had his head stuck on a pole in Plymouth Colony, and his wife and children were sold into slavery in the Bermudas.

More laughter. I went below. By now everyone had gathered on the sunporch. My Uncle Gardner and Aunt Ellen were almost always on the point of hostility—for Ellen's invin-

cible perceptions of what the past had been like
were always being challenged by Gardner's. If
Ellen, as she did now, spoke of old Uncle William Richmond Gardner, who had been master
of his own ship at thirty, who had made a record run from New York to Calcutta, Gardner
reminded her that he had been a difficult man
and had taken a long time dying. Hardly
bested, Ellen brought up the time President
William Howard Taft had come to stay with the
Chaces in 1911, and people had paid attention
to her "because they knew who we were and we
were sure of what we were." At this, my cousin
Lois simply shrugged; at seventeen, she was
ready to cut out. And so, when Ellen recalled
her father's successful campaigns for the Massachusetts Senate, Gardner pointed out that he
had sold the mills to go into politics and at his
death in 1921 there was nothing left but debts.

"Despite all that, we had good times," my
mother said. "We had a lot of fun. I mean, we
shouldn't dwell on the wrong things. I know,
for instance, that the Senator never approved of
me. Why we were like strangers to him, coming
from Poughkeepsie."

"Nor did your mother approve of him," my
father said. "God, how she hated Fall River."

"When she first laid eyes on it in 1914 she
hated it."

"Never made a friend."

"Still hasn't."

These were the facts as my mother re-
ported them: "There were good times then. Between the wars. The time we went out in the
boat and everybody was drinking and we hit
the Mount Hope Bridge and your father jumped
off and swam to shore and later met us at the
yacht club dressed in a white linen suit.

"Remember the time everyone was drinking too much and Charlie Murther fell overboard and drowned and nobody missed him?

"Remember when Shockie's team beat the
original New York Celtics—he was the best
basketball player Fall River ever had, maybe
the best athlete. Before he started drinking too
much. God, Shockie was handsome. And smart.

"Jimmy, your father smelled so much of
horse manure the Senator wouldn't let him into
the house. That's all he cared about. Won a blue
ribbon in the New York Horse Show. Your
brother would remember it. And Lois a little.
And young Gardner a little.

"Of course it changed as time passed. Liquidating mills was the only way your father
could make money. But nowadays I'm afraid
your father is even running out of failed mills."

The Chaces sat down for dinner.

"What happened to the money?" My parents must have asked this question that Fourth

of July in 1944. I asked it thirty years later of
Lois and Gardner. (We had been eating lobsters, and Gardner had brought down a newspaper with the headline: Senator Chace,
Stricken As He Jokes, Dies.) "So, whatever
happened to the money?"

For in 1853, more than fifty years before
the Cotton Centennial, Captain Gardner, the
Senator's uncle, was the owner of the *Monarch
of the Seas,* one of the largest American mer-
chant ships of her time and in the French transport service during the Crimean War. He was a
friend of Nathaniel Hawthorne and visited the
author when he was a consul at Liverpool from
1853 to 1857.

And from his diary: "French Government
to William Gardner, Master, *Monarch of the
Seas,* for carrying troops, 14th May, 1855,
40,012 pounds, 19 shillings, 11 pence." And from
the Bey of Tunis for transporting troops during the Crimean War in 1856: "Stores received
from the Bey as a present, 100 sheep, 15 bul-
locks, 23 jars salt butter, 1,000 pounds sugar,
400 pounds coffee, 10 baskets fruit, 10 baskets
vegetables, 100 fowl, 2,000 eggs, 1,000 loaves
bread, 2 casks olive oil. On passage from Cri-
mea to Marseilles had Colonel of Regiment
aboard, with 400 troops and full band of music,
36 pieces."

"Forty thousand pounds for a shipment of

troops! Then where did the money go?" my
cousin Gardner asked.

"And that's not all," I said.

"On Grandma's side, there was a racetrack
in Central Park," my cousin Lois said.

The Senator's father-in-law, as the obituary
reads, "opened a trotting course known as the
Dubois track. This was the last racetrack constructed on Manhattan Island, and about 1879
the property was taken into Central Park. Mr.
Stephen Dubois received a good price for it and
retired from active business."

"Then what happened to the money?" My
cousins, my aunts, they all asked this question,
with the tone of people who believed that perhaps in some savings bank in New Bedford or
Taunton there was something left. No doubt the
money, what there was of it, went into the Senator's campaigns—a good reason why he was
able to run unopposed for some twenty years.

"He was a friend of labor when labor had
no friend," the obituary reads.

And he saved lobster salad. Truly. In 1906,
to his horror, he discovered a bill that would,
as the *Boston Advertiser* put it, "wipe the lobster salad from the face of the earth." How, you
may well ask, was this to be done? According
to the bill's sponsor, by banning the sale of lobsters or parts of lobsters from the Common-
wealth. "This is the worst yet," said Senator

Chace. "I could stand it when there was a bill planning to protect the heathen or the Mongolian pheasant, but when he makes an attack upon one of our venerable institutions like lobster salad, I revolt."

One could be remembered for less. But they remembered something else on that Fourth of July. They remembered his warning not to let go.

His authority never diminished. Even when my father bridled at his name for his coldness to my mother, there was no escaping him. What he accomplished seemed outsized, though seventy-five years later the stakes may look very small. What he did was willful and cruel and for himself alone. He not only saved lobster salad, he saved his life. In the 1880s there was an epidemic of black diphtheria that struck the city. At that time, my grandmother had six children and he left her in the plague-ridden city with only a little help—and all the children died. A year later my Aunt Sue was born.

As for the money, surely there were campaigns to finance, an ever-larger family to provide for, and the attributes of a statesman to maintain. He gave my father a baby alligator that grew so large they donated it to the city jail. (Why the jail? I imagine the corridors pa-

trolled by an enormous snapping 'gator.) He
also gave my father a chicken, christened Little
Easter, that grew into a hen and was served up
to my father without warning one Sunday afternoon.

All of which makes the Senator out to be
streaked with madness, without redeeming
grace. And yet perhaps not. He was a far-seeing
man. He built the poorhouse at a time when Fall
River was a boomtown. Labeled, then, Chace's
Folly. Yet the poor inhabit it still, and there is a
waiting list for rooms.

A clatter of pebbles in the driveway. I rush
to the window. It was only someone who had
blundered in and left. "Dick's not back yet?" My
mother tries to please.

"You know he won't be back till just before
the fireworks." Aunt Sue states this without
complaint. One can imagine him scurrying between the pinwheels and the rockets. Right
now, just before afternoon dinner with the turkey crackling in the oven, he is standing in a
sand trap or fishing a golf ball out of the creek
next to his thermos of Tom Collins.

"I thought it might be Shockie."

Soon Shockie would drive his dark red
Packard full-tilt down the driveway. Shockie
spoke like W.C. Fields, and I adored him.
("Jimmy, if you want to make a little scratch,

you buy Coke at that American Legion Convention for a nickel and sell it for a dime across the river. You'll make a fortune.")

The board, as it were, groaned. Groans were heard as the turkey, dressing, string beans, acorn squash, crushed cranberries filled up the table. On a hot July day. Dinner like Thanksgiving. "At least your father and mother stood up for us at the wedding."

"What do you mean, Aunt Ellen?" I asked.

"Shockie was supposed to have been an even worse match for the Chaces than your mother, Jimmy. Already he came from what might be described as a shady past. Legends."

"What legends?"

As Ellen explained it then and later, "It began with Lizzie Borden. She killed her parents on the hottest day of August—hot mutton soup for breakfast on that never-to-be-forgotten August day when she gave her father forty-one whacks thinking about what he would think if he discovered the wicked stepmother dead upstairs. I was always told Lizzie gave me a rose in my baby carriage. Or was it an apple? Be that as it may. It was a hot August day, and they were having mutton soup for breakfast, which, I might add, could drive anyone to kill. Anyway, my treasure, it is my opinion that Lizzie did inflict the forty-one whacks on her father— an event which though hard to imagine easily

or even with difficulty—became literally, that
is to say absolutely, incomprehensible when
you think of the circumstances. You see, after
she had killed her stepmother (whom she de-
tested because of the money—it's always the
money, isn't it?—feeling as she did that she was
being done out of her rightful inheritance) she
waited one hour and a half for her father to
come back from lunch. An hour and a half—
alone with the hacked corpse in the upper bedroom. No wonder there were those who thought
the murderer was Bridget the Irish maid who
was supposed to be upstairs resting, though
they say Lizzie paid her off. No one knows for
sure. The private papers of Mr. Jennings the
defense lawyer are still locked up in his attic in
a bathtub.

"Waiting for her father and covered with
blood. And yet when the police discovered Lizzie, though she claims she discovered them,
there was no blood on her dress. Do you think
she was naked? Think of it—Lizzie Borden
took an axe / and gave her mother forty whacks
/ when she saw what she had done / naked she
gave pa forty-one. No wonder he didn't put up
any struggle. Seeing his daughter naked before
him, the axe hid behind her back.

"Of course she paid off the Irish maid. Of
course she had to wait for her father to come
home as it dawned on her that she would have

to murder him so he would not know what she
had done. It makes sense. What doesn't make
sense, or makes sense I can't divine, is that she
stayed on."

And when I asked her what she meant and
where, Ellen explained, as though of course I
should know. "In Fall River. She lived for
thirty-odd years in that city, took the inheritance and built a great house, Maplecroft, in the
Highlands, and stayed on. Can you imagine?
But you have to remember that people thought
she was innocent at first. When she was found
not guilty, the Fall River and Boston and New
York papers hailed the verdict. It was only later
that the schoolboy rhymes sounded outside her
window at Maplecroft. Her sister Emma lived
on with her until the scandal many years after
the murder. It seemed there was an actress she
became involved with. She gave parties for a
troupe of actors and actresses and then, it was
said, she had an involvement. . . . "

"An affair?" Lois asked.

"Who knows? In any case, there was a
fight. Emma left. The actress stayed with Lizzie. And then, can you believe it? Too easily, I
know. And then, Fall River society actually os-
tracized her. You could murder your father and
mother and be given the benefit of the doubt.
But living with another woman—an actress,
moreover—now that was going too far. Poor

Lizzie. She lived alone, finally, at Maplecroft, and left all her money to the Animal Rescue League.

"And Shockie was born in Lizzie's old house. And he found the axe. Or *an* axe. Up the chimney." That was the beginning of Shockie's bravery, Ellen insisted. Living in that house as a little boy.

"If you had known Shockie. The most handsome boy, wasn't he, Mildred?"

"Do you think it's true, Ellen, about that girl committing suicide over him in high school?" my mother asked.

"He married me soon enough after."

"Which means?"

"It may mean he married me because she committed suicide."

"But what about growing up in Lizzie Borden's house?" I asked. "Finding the axe?"

"*An* axe. It was the beginning of his bravery. He was the best basketball player Fall River ever produced. I can remember seeing him the first time at the casino. He looked so slight. But he was fast—whipping in and out, cutting corners, and he was smart as a whip. Maybe, just maybe, if Shockie had become a doctor after college instead of playing football and basketball and roller-hockey, it would have turned out differently for us, for him. I was so alone at night waiting for him to come home when Lois was a baby. Waiting in the flat by the bay. Do you remember it, Lois?"

"No."

"At night listening to the fog horn and waiting for your father. Maybe that's why we got divorced."

"Because you were waiting for my father?"

"Because he couldn't keep up with your wants," Uncle Gardner said.

"My needs, you mean."

"How many pro teams did he own? At his peak?" I asked.

"At his peak? He owned an interest in the Fall River roller-hockey team, and then in the Steamrollers, and finally, in 1935, the track. Lois, you remember that—we used to take you out of school—and in the clubhouse, remember, Shockie always telling you to bet the favorite to place."

"I did that," young Gardner said, "and I lost twenty bucks last week."

"Which shows you still remember your Uncle Shockie's advice. Shockie was a star. The teams started losing when he grew too old to sink a basket from half-court, and then Fall River just couldn't sustain a professional sports team."

Stripped of his teams and later his interest in the racetrack, Shockie passed the war years

in obscure dealings. I use the word advisedly—
obscure dealings—so as not to imply dishon-
esty. Simply to say I do not know. Shockie survived and led what seemed to me a most
glamorous life, when he kept a suite at the Hotel
Mellen. My mother and I would join him for a
drink in the bar. My father would be out cam-
paigning for City Council—a campaign Shockie
was managing—and Mother was lonely, more
than ever after the war, and so we would meet
Shockie for a drink at the bar. He had a gold
cigarette lighter he tossed to the piano player.
But all that took place after the war. His max-
ims live on—bet the favorite to place (as my
daughter did one summer at Saratoga) and you
won't lose too much. The trick, of course, is
betting a long shot to win.

"The trick," Shockie said, "is betting the
favorite to place." It was twilight, and we had
remained on the porch waiting for Uncle Dick
to come home from the country club. Waiting
for the fireworks.

"But, damn it all, Shockie, the favorite usually wins," young Gardner said. Gardner was
too old to be fooled around with. He was
twenty-two and had been in the army even
though he hadn't seen combat and wasn't a hero
like my brother, Hollister, who would have

liked to be with us. Nobody spoke of him. I ached for him to come back so I could see who he had become.

"Well, of course he does," Shockie said. "Of course the favorite usually wins."

"That's why he's the favorite," I said.

"That's why he's the favorite," Shockie said. "But he doesn't pay off much. So why bet on him to win? You cover yourself by betting him to place and, if he wins, you get paid off anyway. But if the long shot is bet on, too, and if the long shot wins, you're on easy street."

My father leaned forward in the wicker chair. "But how are we going to do it, Shockie? How in God's name are we going to do it?"

"It's been easy living for you, Holly, for a long time," Shockie said. "You were born to live that way. But now with the war coming to an end, it won't be so easy anymore. And how are we going to do it? Buy for a nickel, sell for a dime?"

It was then they concocted the scheme of running my father for City Council, and then for Mayor. After the fighting was over and the last gasp of the wartime boom gone, there would be no more cotton mills in Fall River, and a long shot could win. Meaning my father. Who was not such a long shot, after all, with the

Chace name and his son Hollister a war hero who would stand next to him on the platform wearing his Bronze Star and his Purple Heart.

The idea came in a rush, like the fireworks themselves that were to come later that night. Who thought of it first hardly matters. Though it was surely my father himself, reaching into the dying light to seize upon the one thing that would redeem time wasted. Shockie, rising from his chair and pulling us with him, explained how we would all be cut into the deal, and how it would restore to us what we had lost after the First World War. Ellen was with us. She would campaign like the old fury. And Sue would bankroll it—for who else could they turn to now?

Even my mother held back only a little, skittish only a little. But she had, after all, married a Chace, and so she would be dragged forward, willy-nilly. What else could she do? Shockie, whom she trusted, an outsider like herself, would cajole her and comfort her, and there was nothing to fear, nothing to lose, it was no big deal, and her husband would not be lost to her as he now was with his idleness and philandering.

"I will," she said, "become the good campaigner."

• •

It was a year after that Fourth of July that
Shockie stood on the window seat of his suite at
the Mellen Hotel, mobilizing us for the campaign. His energy came forth in laughter and
whispers. You would have thought it was the
Mayor's race already. First, the pep talk, then
walking around the room, his hand on someone's shoulder or even kneeling at my mother's
feet pleading with her softly, softly: "We'll win,
Mildred, I promise."

After the primaries there were only three
men still in the race for the district. On the wall
a map of Fall River was already tacked up, thick
crayoned lines marking out the wards.

"Do you think a Yankee can still win?
You've got the Highlands. But for the rest of the
wards—with Dumas and Silvia running—I
wonder." Uncle Gardner was never optimistic.
In any case, he was going to California by Labor
Day to start up a new business. He would be no
use to us then.

Ellen was dressed in white with a long
pearl strand. It was as though she were ready
to go to a garden party, and when Shockie
walked past her, she would reach out to him,
her hand touching his sleeve. My mother
hummed; she stroked her throat. Her nerves
were bad now—my brother would not be home
that summer either, unless the war in the Pacific ended. If only she were less anxious. For

here was a last chance for my father to make it all good. She was humming—a phrase from a song called "Throw Out the Lifeline."

On that afternoon, with the heat rising from the river and no fans in the hotel room, my father was the only one of us to move swiftly, nod his head to ratify a decision, and smile only faintly at Shockie's gibes. Finally, he seemed ruthless enough to win.

Shockie moved to the map. "It begins here at the beach. And do you know why? Because we have to work for the Mayor as well—we'll need his support—and that's not easy. On the next July day at Horseneck Beach, walking between the cookouts and the kids sprawled out in the sand and God knows what else—a stud in the sand dunes and grandma baking like a lobster—there you'll go, eating as they say a peck of dirt before you die, and shaking hands with the working class. Every Sunday till Labor Day you'll work the district and young Gardner and Lois and Jimmy will work the beach. Even Ellen will work it—the higher class in the cabanas, of course." Then he paused and smiled at my mother. "Not you, though. Your skin's too fair."

"And in the evening," my father said, "when the tide comes in—or goes out—and only a few stragglers are left, I'll take a swim."

Shockie nodded. "I'll meet you afterwards

for a drink at the Inn, right at the point. We can add up the score. Just look at this goddamn city —Gaul divided into three parts." He walked over to the map. "The French are here, starting from the reservoir and running down Bedford Street. It gets sort of raggedy near Hartwell Street, a few old Cockneys and whatever else has been tossed up. Then moving north— you've got Ruggles Park and Sacred Heart—the nuns and priests are everywhere, so watch yourself. It's enough to make a man like me run for cover."

In the heat, my mother's fan beating gently, the soft coolness.

"What do you want me to do?" I asked.

"You and young Gardner and Lois can be working the playgrounds. A vote for your dad means a new swing or a basketball hoop. Get to the kids and you'll get to the fathers and mothers. You can infiltrate the tennis courts. Make a friend who's batting his brains out on the asphalt. By Labor Day you'll be an ace at the net. And then, come Labor Day, we'll hit the Highlands. They're your kind. Where else can they go?"

In 1945, there were still half a dozen or so cotton mills left, and at the changing of the shifts at six in the morning, my father and I would be there, he shaking hands, I handing out leaflets. One morning we stood opposite my great-grandfather's mill which had become an outlet for discount auto parts.

"Is this your boy?"

"It is."

"Did you ever work in a mill, kid?"

"No."

"You can't hear afterwards."

"We need to replace the old looms," my father said.

"And what's to take its place?" The mill-hand laughed softly.

"New looms, new industry."

"You believe that?"

My father also believed that he was one of them. He had known mills since he was born, and his ease with these men was astounding to me. How do you learn to live so directly? The question plagued me then and it plagues me still.

"I have to work the mills," he said. "They won't trust my name."

The war was just over, and relief was mixed with apprehension. If there were boom times ahead—and few men in 1945 believed there would be—even fewer in Fall River believed it. What need there was during the war for cotton cloth would most likely end. We stalked the mills and thought the same and did not say so.

"It's a no-win game," Shockie said. "I don't

mean we can't win—but promise them nothing."

"Which will get us nothing."

"Don't you bet on it. Remember the old
Senator—a friend of labor when labor had no
friend."

My father laughed and nodded sagely. "He
built the poorhouse. Chace's Folly, now that's a
friend."

Best of all were the night rallies when I
could stand backstage or in the corner of a bar-
room. But rally is too extreme a word for what
took place. It was setting up the bar for drinks
—"Holly's buying"—and looking down the long
mahogany bar saying a few words. It was
mostly low key, because there was not much
you could say that sounded honest to working
men of that ilk. No one believed in any brighter
future. Apprehension was the most accurate
way to describe it. Their fear for the loss of
their jobs had not yet surfaced—we were still
too near the war—just the nagging suspicion
that time was running out, the city had become
a remnant. "The problem is not unemploy-
ment," my father said.

"Not yet."

"Well, it soon will be."

"Yes," my father said. "It soon will be. No
one's been thinking about what's going to happen after the war. The payoff is going to come,

and you know it, and I know it, and there's not much time left." He could talk to them in this way, for there was not much else to offer them.

Which is why he would win. At the Belmont Club it was the conventional wisdom. "Silvia and Dumas—the Portugees and the Canucks—divide the votes between them, and Holly gets the Irish, the Yankees and the whole claptrap who don't want one of their own, knowing what one of your own always does to you."

The Belmont Club behind the hotel was, in fact, not a club, but a bar for politicians. After the war my brother would be a regular, buying drinks for the house. The last of the big spenders. At the Belmont Club they spoke of him, now sick with malaria in the Philippines. "Hollister—now there's a politician for you."

"Jimmy, you remember how tough he was?"

"No, I don't really."

"I always liked Hollister."

"I hardly remember him," I said. "I know it sounds crazy. I've only got pieces of him. Letters. A baseball cap."

"I never remember his playing baseball."

"Maybe he never did. But I've got his baseball cap."

"He used to wear it to the Red Sox games. What a heartbreaker they were. Still are, for that matter. Doerr, Williams, Dom DiMaggio, they'll never win no matter who they've got. Much Better Than His Broth-er Joe / Is Dom-in-ic Di-Mag-gi-o."

"My father will win, won't he?"

"I don't think they'll let a Portugee in, not yet. A Frenchman maybe. Anyway, once Holly's elected, Shockie will see to it he's re-elected. And then he'll run for Mayor."

"Don't lose the faith, Jimmy. You might be a senator yourself some day. But I'll tell you something. You've got to want it more than anything. And keep wanting it."

Going to the funeral home was almost a daily stop in the campaign. But Protestant wakes were hardly wakes at all. In the funeral home the tone was properly somber, with feelings suddenly gone out of kilter.

"We're waking him tonight, Holly."

"I'll be by."

It was Timmy Winslow's wake that may have been one of the turning points in the campaign.

Ward Nine. Tuesday night. We were standing in the outer room with the widow, poor Sophie Winslow, who trembled but never wept. My father was trying to explain to Sophie what sadness lay in his heart. He and Timmy had been cadets in high school during the first war.

Then, after the war, Timmy lived opposite the Historical Society until he got a job as the curator, setting up the old rooms where the bookcase led to the Underground Railway. He used to show me the breastplate of the Viking skeleton in armor.

Suddenly Sophie gave out a little cry. My father quickly supported her. But she wasn't looking at the gray casket. In the doorway half a dozen men in American Legion hats, holding paper poppies, stood stiffly. "It's the veterans," she said, stricken.

"I know," my father said. "I'd forgotten he was in the army."

"He was only in for two months. In 1918. The war ended before he got his commission. He never got out of Boston."

"Thank God."

Marching into the room, Marty Milligan grasped my father's hand and said to Sophie, "We've come."

"But he never even joined the Legion," she said.

"It don't matter." He sighed. "She's upset, Chace."

"What's the problem?"

"Well, it's a lovely thing," Marty said. "We're going to march in, and there's a spoken prayer, and each vet leaves a poppy on the coffin. Don't take ten minutes."

"Sophie?" my father asked.

"Any veteran's entitled," Marty went on. "You'll see now. It's beautiful. You can be any religion."

Sophie began to sob. My father supported her as six men stomped in and stood before Timmy's coffin, their heads bowed. . . . "Another buddy has been called to meet the Supreme Commander. . . . Bless the ones here today who call him buddy, and help us to be as brave as we were on the fields of battle. . . . Farewell, our buddy, farewell." Each vet laid a red crepe poppy on the coffin, then turned smartly and left the room. The last, Marty himself, leaned close to the widow and whispered: "They ought to have draped the casket with the flag."

"He never served ninety days. He never got out of Boston. We don't need the flag."

"You've got a flag. The Legion always gives the widow a flag." Marty produced Old Glory, folding it in a triangle, and, with no warning to Sophie, whipped it over the casket like a busboy setting the table.

"There, Sophie."

By now she was weeping openly in my father's arms while Marty saluted the coffin. "Always moves them, the ceremony," said Marty. "He went the best way."

For the rest of the evening Marty stayed in

the corner and said nothing, just looking at the flag, and that night my father and I stayed to the end, too. Sophie was forlorn, and so we took charge of greeting the mourners. It was time to go before we noticed Marty hadn't left. "It's time, Marty," my father said.

"There's one thing, Holly. You could explain to Sophie," Marty said. "There's this development-housing for the old folks—and I figured Sophie would want to donate the flag here as a memorial to Tim here. It's a big thing. The Mayor—the old Mayor, Holly, will be there, and I thought it would be something fitting and decent to commemorate Tim here. So . . . if I could just take the flag now—"

"You can't have it." As my father said this, he turned away and pulled Sophie after him.

"What do you mean? It's to be a memorial. And the Winslow name—what will they think?"

"I mean," my father said, his voice rising, "I mean you can't have it. And I don't care whether she wanted it or not. I know what these things cost, and I know you'll be pocketing the twelve bucks you'll get for the flag. You people go to the widow before the coffin is even in the ground and ask for the flag. Beautiful. I know all the tricks, Marty. I know all about the twelve bucks and the flag—what Sophie here doesn't know."

"I don't want to know," Sophie said.

"You hear?" my father shouted. "You can't have the flag."

"What will they think of the Winslows?"

"It doesn't matter," Sophie said. "It doesn't matter what they think. He never served his ninety days. He never got a pension. He never got the disability. He never got a bonus. He never left Boston—he hardly made it out of Fall River."

My father showed Marty out of the room and led Sophie to the limousine.

Which, as I figure it, is how we lost the Legion vote.

Hot October. The leaves fell late in an endless Indian summer. Less than a month to go before the election. At Lincoln Park the Textile Workers of America held their Columbus Day Clambake and, along with the Mayor, my father and Dumas were to speak. Did it make such a difference? Shockie thought so. "They remember. The point is they remember."

My father said, "I'll tell them Fall River is dying."

"It will make them choke on their quahogs."

After my father and mother first met at Lincoln Park in 1917, he courted her in the dance hall, on the merry-go-round—"I'll catch the ring." He must have leaned far, far out, and

there, the middle finger like a boat hook, he
caught the ring. He was always graceful on a
horse.

In 1945, Lincoln Park had grown tougher.
On Saturday, the crowds that wandered among
the Whip, the Snake, and the Cat O'Nine Tails
could turn ugly. A sudden fist fight. The smash
of a putter across a man's shoulder could turn
the miniature golf course into shambles. And
people drove the Dodgems at each other like
tanks. It was as though the war had shrunk to
this little cage.

For the Columbus Day outing, the clams
and the ears of corn were being cooked in seaweed between the shooting galleries and the
pinball arcade. The sun burned like July. In the
distance the roller coaster raced along its track.
A small boy cried because he was lost. I walked
between the benches handing out leaflets, fairly
lost myself. Shockie was nowhere. Young Gardner and Lois had wandered away. The sound
man loped by me with a microphone and a couple of speakers. I saw the other candidate on a
bench chomping his ear of corn. In half an hour,
just after the noon whistle, the speeches were
to begin. Then, suddenly, like waves breaking,
Shockie's shouts came at me from the top of the
Flying Carpet.

Ducking under the roller coaster, I made
my way toward him; but even this apparent

short cut took longer than I had imagined, for
the scaffolding made a maze out of the under-
pinnings of the track. Shockie was kneeling on
top of the Carpet slide by the time I stood below
looking up at him, some fifty feet above me.
"Your father," he cried.

"Father?"

The long shrieking train started its de-
scent. I could hear nothing but the cries of pas-
sengers and the roar of the cars. And then it
passed and the air was still. Shockie's voice
dropped. "Your father. Where is he?"

I remembered Dumas eating his corn, and
about to plunge into a bowl of steamed clams.
The picnickers were readying themselves for
the Columbus Day speeches, irritated that they
should have to listen, yet bound to the scheme
of things, expecting and requiring the candidates to make their pitch. It was like the factory
handshakes. Did anyone want to be disturbed
by a stranger at daybreak?

"Find him."

Shockie had lost control. Here he was
standing like a ninny on top of an enormous
children's slide, trying to seek out my father in
the crowd. I ran between the Ferris wheel and
the Fun House, batting away autumn flies, cir-
cling the amusement park until I found our
empty car. Then I began the search through the
arcades, farther and farther away from the

union picnic. How like a summer's day, sailors and soldiers out of uniform, in their chino pants with their severance pay to spend.

I found them at last—my mother and father—she sitting quite still on the far side of the carousel and my father walking quickly back and forth in front of her, then stopping, holding her hand, squatting beside her. Something in the way they behaved stopped me. The merry-go-round must have been broken, for the turntable was silent and no one was there, and so I came upon them like a pathfinder with all the practical stealth I had learned by playing at spies. I lay in the lap of a chariot and listened to him.

"I could have gone to Shanghai years ago," he was saying. "I should have known I was missing the chance to get out of Fall River. Marrying hardly a day after Armistice Day, it was so hard to know what to do with my life."

"I don't think I can go on with the campaign, Holly."

"I know."

"You know what I'm like. I can't do these public things."

She was silent.

"Mildred?"

Still nothing.

"Mildred?"

She drifted. "We could still go away," he

went on. "It would be like your mother's stories
—where we'd live. Along the Hudson, up from
the Palisades, Bear Mountain. A clean slate, I'm
only forty-seven, a young man, right? Look at
Gardner, off to California, and he's almost fifty.
We could go—not as far as Poughkeepsie, but
far enough. Take risks." He paused. "I promise."

"No, please. You used to promise we'd go
away. No more promises."

"It will be different this time."

"You don't understand, Holly. Promise not
to say that we'll go. Just promise that."

"But I promise that I will go. That's the
point."

"No, I need just a little more time to get
used to things."

"Trust me."

"Just a little more time. Please, Holly. Just
a little more time."

Far away someone was crying his name,
and there he was holding her now, rocking back
and forth. She was still pleading for more time
and did he understand?

I must have come at them like a bowling
ball. "Shockie wants you. It's late." You grab at
your parents, trying not to let them slip away.
Monstrous pull of a boy. "It's late."

By the time my father reached the platform, Dumas had finished his speech and the

restless crowd was beginning to drift away. New piles of corn on the cob were steaming in the sun. What was politics on the verge of an Indian summer too hot to be believed? Foaming beer and clam cakes, the seaweed smell of the baking. I saw my father weaving in the sun as he spoke. "Fall River is dying. But it doesn't have to. It's not fate. Do any of you remember what it was like after the First World War? The recession we never pulled out of? And what happened—even in the booming twenties, there was no boom for us, and there's no boom ahead —it will be too late the next time.

"Bankruptcy. You remember—the city sent into the hands of a court-appointed state commission to set our house in order. Do you want to hear the facts again?"

The facts, the figures, the promises seemed to be lost among the hands reaching out for ears of corn or a pitcher of beer. Was my mother crying? Where was Shockie? The crowd was all around me.

"I want a drink," someone said.

"My God in Heaven, this city *is* dying," said another.

"Who cares?" someone asked.

I fled. The bus was packed with merry-makers. We lurched through the narrow lane between the elm trees, down to the rim of the bay. To the left was Rattlesnake Hill, a slab of rock set high above the scrub grass of the marshy fields. I got off the bus before the summer houses began and ran to a farmyard near the railroad bridge. There, under the shadow of the black girders, the boat Aunt Sue had bought me turned at the mooring. Over the Hummocks, across the river, the day's-end wind was coming up: I could see a cabana, its striped canvas slapping against the poles. A crab fisherman scooped the water with his net, then looked past the slate hills to watch the wind send a seagull above the path from the channel.

In the boathouse, I pulled on a field jacket like my brother's and, without bothering to check the sail for battens, loaded my arms with the rudder, boom, and canvas. I looped the skiff's painter over the stone and ran down to the beach, then pushed off so quickly my chino pants were soaked to the knees. I even rigged the boat without bothering to see if the mainsail was pulled taut.

The catboat tacked easily under the railroad bridge, and I saw the city eastward where the river became a bay, granite factories silver in the sunlight. Buoys tolled, and the black channel marker loomed above the bow like a derelict. The sail luffed in the quickening breeze. I pulled in the sheet line to my stomach until the canvas belled out, waited for the tension in my arms and legs to go, waited for my

eye to seek out a landmark or seamark to set a
course by, and to feel free. The boat swung on
its tack, away from the city toward the cove and
the islands.

I imagined my father sitting now at the
table over coffee and my mother glancing back
and forth, right and left, to the empty places left
by her two sons. First Hollister, and now
Jimmy. Would Hollister ever come back? If
only he, not I, had been there at the clambake,
if only he had stood on the platform in his med-
als, if only he had come back and not deserted
us, if only he had died in the war—in a cave in
the Philippines, on a beach where the tide came
up to wash his body deeper into the sand, in a
burst of shellfire over his foxhole, at night on a
march through the undergrowth by a sniper's
bullet. I knew all the instants of death.

The waves rolled higher now, against and
over the prow, sending a chill spray against my
army jacket. I came about through the Hummocks and into the cove where the water was
still, a thicker green, with minnows swarming
in the wake of the rudder. On the two small
islands the beaches narrowly rimmed the
thicket of birches, willows, ivy and grape vines,
raspberry bushes which stopped only a few
yards from the water. Glazed by sunlight, the
thicket steamed; the leaves were not the usual
Fall River mossy green or yellow from spindrift,

but green as the tropical islands that I had
never seen. I imagined hearing a parrot caw
while I let the boat run downward toward the
shore, the breeze so gentle that I could leave
the tiller, pull up the centerboard, and wait for
the bow to scrape the sand. Here the water was
blue and clear: the sandy bottom showed star-
fish, blue-shell crabs, seaweed fixed like coral.
I thought of the Pacific.

On the beach at last, I lay on the sand that
was pocked with holes made by fiddler crabs;
then stirred, lifted my head, squinted across
the island as though I expected to see eyes peer-
ing through the ferns, the silver steel flash of a
rifle barrel, and falling from the arm of a palm
tree my brother head first, somersaulting in the
air and landing in a sprawl on the shore. The
blood from Hollister's mouth ran on the sand;
his hand held sand as he slipped back to the
tidemarks. *I'm sorry, Hollister. God, forgive me.*
I wanted to lie on my back and let my brother
hit me and hit me until he was too tired to go
on. My father had worn a broad-brimmed hat
and puttees and spent his war in a New England
camp, while Hollister had seen his entire pla-
toon killed and had been wounded in the thigh
on the beach and fallen in the bloody sand and
water.

I felt a shadow come over me and looked
up to see the sun broken by leaves. Gulls sailed

close to me. I stood up, shaking the wet sand
from my pants as the boat turned listlessly at
the end of the painter. The tide was coming in.
A driftwood skiff was overturned, and cobwebs
arched out from the keel like cocoons. Wreck-
age on the bay side was common: I'd already
found hats, oil drums, army boots swept into
the cove through the riptide twice a day. Now I
saw new flotsam piled high against the spiny
bush. The stenciled block lettering on the boxes
and duffle bags would have meant a ship had
been torpedoed, but the war was over now,
maybe the debris had been simply jettisoned by
the crew of a wrecked cargo ship and washed
up in the cold to dry in the sun. I pressed my
hands on the wood: it was still damp. With a
rock too blunt for a chisel, I dug at the board,
but after five minutes my hands were sore while
the wood lay unbroken. The duffle bag was easier. One blow broke the rusty lock, and when I
dumped it out there were piles of olive-drab
army underwear.

Feeling like Crusoe, with my hair straggly,
I stood in my chino pants, slipped on the field
jacket, then jammed on my head an army over-
seas cap I found in the duffle bag. Giant step-
ping along over the sand, I clenched my teeth
against the hail of bullets, diving and bellying
across the pebbles on elbows and knees, rifle
cradled in my arms. It was the way that Hollis-

ter had taken, crablike, along the beaches, through hot sunlight till the sun disappeared, and the light grew weak as fog, and the sea, as it did now, tarnished.

Through the gap, across the bay, Fall River rose darkly. I stripped off the jacket and cap and walked slowly along the shore to the boat. Cast off, free of sandbars, the sails stretching with the wind, the boat came about in the running tide, and from the stern I saw the island in the dusky light, no longer green and lush and steaming with tropical blossoms, but as pale as the sand dunes by the ocean, with dry stunted branches and gray brush, the island I had known for years to have a cookout on or go skinny dipping from, the island as familiar as my street.

I was late. The sunlight was almost gone, the waves grew high and the water darker, and to get back to the boathouse and catch a bus for home would make it after dark, make my father angry. So what did it matter about the bullets skimming the water, or the sniper in the palm trees, or the body on the beach holding sand in his fist, what did it matter—it was all the war. The war got you off scot free: you kill, you steal, you hurt your brother, you kill your father, it's all the war.

Next to the centerboard lay the field jacket. I tied the sheetline around the cleat, leaned forward, pressed the tiller with my knees and sliding it along my leg, steered with my bare foot. Then I stripped off my chino pants to my swim trunks, took the jacket and cap in my arms and threw the clothes overboard. They floated at first, then with a gusty, scaling wind, the cap peaked, the arms of the jacket and the legs of the pants stretched out over the water. The boat rolled in the waves, shivered and fell, and rose up again, while I hung over the gunwale, my throat so tight I could hardly breathe, looking at the scarecrow of my soldier brother caught and pulled down into the sea.

Election night at our house: 1945. And Aunt Sue was there. For years they had come to her because she was the only one who had succeeded and symbolized for them the moral force that her success lent her. Had she not married Dick Hawkins, she might have been reduced to wheedling demands like Holly and Gardner, or to posturing like Ellen, who had always envied her. The Senator had loved her best, indeed she had been his confidante. At the time of his death, Sue was the surest witness of some past no one quite remembered. And with Dick's money she held them in the grip of her own mythology. The myth, of course, was character, character that the Chaces had presumably once possessed and that was being passed

through her to Lois and young Gardner and
Hollister and me.

The night her brother was to be elected to
the City Council she told us about the Senator's
last campaign. Just before he died, they had
gone off to Martha's Vineyard. On the island,
he was waiting for her at the dock, and then
came the fast carriage ride through the dusk
and the two of them late in the night in a house
in Chilmark: "That's when he told me that he
had to win the election. The last of the mills we
had any interest in were due to close unless he
won. We were alone the weekend before the
election. I wondered why he'd asked me to
come—maybe he'd had a premonition of his
death. Holly had just started in the mill and
expected to get control of it. They work sixty
hours a week in the South, Holly told me. And
the South's machinery is newer.

"I more or less knew that anyway. What I
didn't know was what my father told me about
his plan. You see, there was an excess profits
tax passed at the end of the war, but the mill
owners hadn't enough put aside to pay it. All
those wonderful years during the war, all the
lovely dividends, endless profits for personal
pleasure—and nothing left. Nothing left to replace the worn-out machinery, the Senator told
me, no cash reserves. 'Now you listen to me,

Sue'—he was that worried, unlike him, so cock-
sure you know—'I told the General Manager
not to put a nickel aside for the new machines.
The profits we made—and they were enormous
—are being used for this campaign. That's why
the organization is working the way it is. *I'm*
paying the bills, not any party committee. It's
my money and I've got to win.'

" 'But if you win,' I said, 'you'll buy new
looms.' And then he turned on me. It was
darker now, and I was scared a little. 'If I win,'
he said, '*I'll* decide whether to buy new machines or whether it's too late to bother with
that. We can go on using the old machines for a
while longer. But whichever way I decide, that
mill is going to get contracts. Like an old ship,
we'll run it into the grave if need be.'

"When I asked if Holly knew, he said, no,
he couldn't risk his son's knowing he couldn't
afford to replace a single loom now. 'I don't
trust my sons, Gardner *or* Holly.' That's just
how he said it. 'And anyway,' he said, 'I may
decide that all Fall River's cotton mills will fail,
that the future lies with the South, after all. And
if that's the way it's going to be, then better
Holly shouldn't know that some day soon those
mills will have to be liquidated, and the only
important thing is to keep repairing the looms,
making do with every trick I know until there's

no profit to be made and no contracts that even
I can get hold of. But if I tell him to go South
because the risk is too great to stay here and
the decision to keep operating will always be
mine, then Holly will have to know why. He'll
find out that there are debts to be paid off and
that what was coming in was for my use alone,
for my campaign. But then,' he said, 'I might
replace the old looms, after all, and then he'd
lose nothing.'

"Well, he was right, you know. If he wasn't
going to decide what to do with the mill till after
the election, he was right Holly shouldn't know.
So he told me instead. And then I had to keep
the secret. He wanted my complicity, and I gave
it to him. He told me, 'I don't want you to lose
anything, but I want you to know the world as
it is. I want you to know just what it takes to
live as we live.'

"Well, he won that election. And then he
died so sudden I don't know what he would
have done. The mills had to go, because, like he
said, the money was all tied up and the debts
were so great, and yet here's Holly tonight after
all these years, he might be the Mayor yet."

That night, after Sue's story, there were
only votes to be counted, tallies according to
wards and precincts. We got the results first by
radio. Young Gardner took down the totals

from the wards and then Lois labeled them, and
we all sat waiting for my father and Shockie to
come back to us.

"We've won six precincts so far and lost
only two," young Gardner said.

Sue was silent now, and even Ellen waited
quietly, once in a while touching my mother's
arm, either to reassure her that she would lose
nothing or simply because she was afraid they
were losing. It seemed hours without any conversation, just Lois giving out the figures. All
those charts no one could decipher but Shockie
and my father, and when they arrived, they
hardly said hello, just went to the tables and
looked at the returns. It took them only a few
minutes.

"The hell."

"The Portuguese wards," my father said. "I
didn't think he'd take them."

"We should have known after the Columbus Day picnic."

"What else could I have done? Time ran out
on us, Shockie. We just couldn't make it up."

Then my mother went over to him. "Yes,
we needed more time. That was all we needed,
Holly." My father looked at her. He seemed bewildered. Then he smiled, and looked beyond
her. She went on, "It was Steve Gazely's fault,
wasn't it? You know what I mean, Jimmy? No?

Well, Hollister would remember if he were here. Whenever something went wrong, it was because of Steve Gazely. If I was dealt a bad hand of cards, it was Steve Gazely must've shuffled them. If it weren't for Steve Gazely, we could have won those wards, and it would've made all the difference."

Our false friend, our nemesis—there never was a Steve Gazely.

It was finally dark at Aunt Sue's on that Fourth of July in 1944 when Hollister was still away and hope kept breaking in.

In the garden below, Uncle Dick had started the fireworks. They came slowly at first —the pinwheels, the fountains—and the trees glistened. If only it would go on and on, rockets rising above the willow trees and breaking far out over the river. The stars fell between masts and spars. In the darkness on the porch the family stood together, as though we were afraid something would catch fire and the falling stars of the fireworks might never go out. Lines of light like tracer bullets.

At last, the rockets and roman candles grew dim. In the garden, Uncle Dick was walking up the stairs with enormous sparklers for the children, and I heard my father singing, first in little more than a hum, then louder, braver—

*As I walked along the Bois de Bologne*
*With an independent air*
*You could hear the boys declare*
*Why he's a millionaire . . .*
*For he's the man who broke the bank*
*At Monte Carlo.*